# The Black Peoples of America

**DOUGLAS R FEATONBY**

## Hodder Murray

A MEMBER OF THE HODDER HEADLINE GROUP

# Acknowledgements

## To Jean, for all her support.

The front cover shows Sojourner Truth reproduced courtesy of © Bettmann/Corbis, and Martin Luther King Jr marching with a crowd in the March Against Fear through rural Mississippi, June 1966, reproduced courtesy of © Flip Schulke/Corbis.

The publishers would like to thank the following individuals, institutions and companies for permission to reproduce copyright illustrations in this book:

Actionplus/Glyn Kirk p45 (right); AP Photo p41 (right); AP Photo/Bill Hudson p36 (bottom); AP Photo/Byrd Family Photo p44 (bottom left); AP Photo/Charles Rex Arbogast p45 (bottom); AP Photo/Gene Herrick, p30; AP Photo/HO p44 (bottom centre); AP Photos/KTLA p44 (top); AP Photo/Perry Aycock p35; AP Photo/S.F. Examiner page 43l; Associated Press page 36 (top); Associated Press/Jackson Daily News/Fred Blackwell page 34; Associated Press/Sam Mircovich/Pool page 44 (right); Ben Buxton/Anti-Slavery International page 3 (bottom); Bettmann/Corbis pages 2, 11, 19, 22 (top right), 27 (top right), 27 (centre left), 28, 31, 40 (right), 42 (bottom left), 43 (top right), 49 (bottom left); © Bradley Smith/Corbis p26tl; *Koranna Hottentots Preparing to Move* by Samuel Daniell, 1805, Cape Town Archives Repository page 9 (bottom right), (Ref # M1054); © Corbis pages 7, 15, 18, 22 (centre top), 24, 26 (top right), 42 (right); David Edwards p9 (top left); Flip Schulke/Corbis pages 26 (bottom right), 27 (top left), 27 (bottom), 43 (bottom); Hulton Archive page 26 (centre); Hulton-Deutsch Collection/Corbis pages 40 (left), 42 (top left); Hulton Getty page 26 (bottom left); Hulton Getty page 41 (left); Leif Skoogfors/Corbis page 45 (top left); Leonard de Selva/Corbis page 10; Mary Evans Picture Library pages 3 (top), 22 (bottom left); New York Public Library page 6; Oscar White/Corbis page 22 (top left); Paul Almasy/Corbis pages 8 (top), 9 (top right); Peter Newark's American Pictures page 23; Peter Newark's Historical Pictures page 9 (centre right); Robert Holmes/Corbis page 13; © Topham Picturepoint page 27 (centre right); Werner Forman Archive pages 4 (bottom), 8 (bottom).

The publishers would also like to thank the following for permission to reproduce material in this book:

Extracts from *Strange Fruit*, words and music by Lewis Allan, reproduced with the permission of Carlin Music Corporation; Julius Lester for the extracts from *To Be a Slave* by J Lester, Puffin Books, 1968.

Every effort has been made to trace and acknowledge ownership of copyright. The publishers will be glad to make suitable arrangements with any copyright holders whom it has not been possible to contact.

Orders: please contact Bookpoint Ltd, 130 Milton Park, Abingdon, Oxon OX14 4SB. Telephone: (44) 01235 827720, Fax: (44) 01235 400454. Lines are open from 9.00 – 6.00, Monday to Saturday, with a 24 hour message answering service. You can also order through our website at www.hoddereducation.co.uk

*British Library Cataloguing in Publication Data*
A catalogue record for this title is available from The British Library

ISBN-10: 0 340 79034 2
ISBN-13: 978 0 340 79034 2

First published 2001
Impression number          10 9 8 7
Year                                  2005

Copyright © 2001 Douglas Featonby and Martyn Whittock

Typeset by Liz Rowe
Printed in Italy for Hodder Murray, an imprint of Hodder Education, a member of the Hodder Headline Group, 338 Euston Road, London NW1 3BH by Printer Trento.

# Contents

# 1 SLAVERY COMES TO THE AMERICAS

## THIS CHAPTER ASKS
What is freedom?
What is slavery?
How were slaves captured and transported to the Americas?
How were slaves sold in America?

## NEW WORDS

**CIVILISATION:** a highly developed and organised society.
**DEMOCRACY:** a country where the people elect their leaders and have many freedoms.

## FREEDOM TO ... FREEDOM FROM ...

We live in a **democracy** where young people and adults enjoy many freedoms. Some are freedoms to do certain things. Some are freedoms which protect us from bad treatment. Throughout history, however, millions of people have not enjoyed such freedoms – because they were slaves. Slaves were present in the ancient **civilisations** of Egypt, Greece and Rome and, in fact, at one time or another could be found in many parts of Europe, Asia, Africa and the Americas. Unfortunately, in some parts of the world, a form of slavery exists, even today.

## TO BE A SLAVE

To be a slave is to be owned by another person – just as a computer might be owned by you – or a car might be owned by your parents. In other words a slave is classed as property. Some slaves in the past were not even allowed basic information about themselves. Many were brutally treated.

## MOTIVES FOR SLAVERY

A slave works for nothing – and so is a source of very cheap labour. Many were forced to work in the fields, producing crops such as cotton and sugar, while others were used as servants. Some were craftspeople who made items for sale such as leather goods and jewellery. Another motive for slavery lay in the fact that some people believed they were superior to others and had a right to enslave them.

## SOURCE A

The slave was regarded and treated as a work animal. The slave-owner could, at any moment, sell a mother from her child, a husband from his wife.

▲ *Julius Lester, a Black American historian (1968).*

## SOURCE B

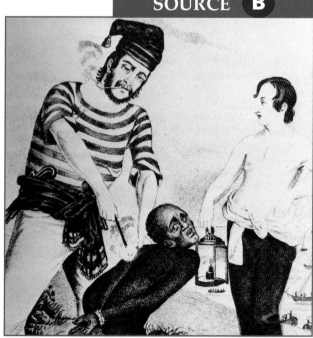

▲ *Branding of a slave with a mark showing the owner. From a 19th-century illustration.*

## HOW PEOPLE BECAME SLAVES

Many were captured in war. In Africa, for example, some tribes constantly fought each other and prisoners were sold as slaves. People might be enslaved as punishment for a crime; others were kidnapped. Some, however, agreed to become slaves to escape poverty and starvation. Many were born into slavery – and while it may seem strange, there were times when people were sold as slaves, by parents, other relatives, or even the person they were married to!

### SOURCE C

They whipped my Father 'cause he looked at a slave they killed, and cried.

▲ *Roberta Manson, a Black slave in America.*

### SOURCE D

▲ *Breaking up soil in the sugar plantations, 19th century.*

### SOURCE E

The White folk was beating the niggers, burnin' and boilin' 'em.

▲ *Alice Johnson, a Black slave in America.*

### SOURCE F

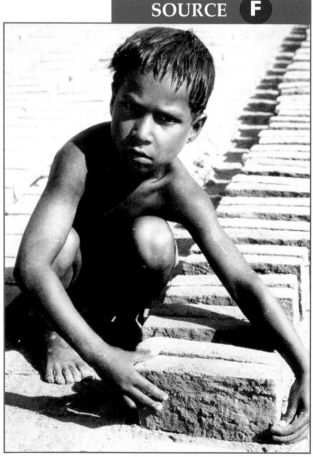

▲ *A modern child-slave, making bricks in Pakistan.*

According to ANTI-SLAVERY INTERNATIONAL, in the Middle East today, some children under 7 are sold as camel jockeys.

**Q**

**1.** How free are you? List some of the things that you are free to do. What bad things are you free from?

**2.** Design two spidergrams to show: the motives for slavery in the past *and* how people became slaves.

**3.** 'Slaves are not treated as human beings. They are seen as property.' Explain how the sources show this is true.

**Discussion Point**
Can you think of any basic freedoms you believe all people should have? List them.

## SLAVERY IN AFRICA

In the Middle East, in the 7th century AD, the Arabs, spurred on by the new religion of **Islam**, began to build an empire, which would eventually include parts of Europe and Northern Africa. The Arabs wanted slaves for this empire but were forbidden by the **Koran** to enslave their own people. They were forced to look elsewhere. The solution to the problem lay in Africa. There, powerful tribes, such as the Berbers, kept slaves, as did the mighty kingdoms of Songhay and Mandingo. In the city state of Kano, food was produced by forced labour. Africa, therefore, was able to provide the slaves the Arabs wanted. Slaves in Africa, however, could look forward to being freed eventually – if they worked hard and caused no trouble.

## THE EUROPEANS AND THE AFRICAN SLAVE TRADE

Some African states on the West Coast were separated from the main trade routes, which crossed the Sahara Desert, by dense forest, and so they began to look to a new source of trade – the Europeans. From the early 15th century the Portuguese began to explore the coast of Africa and, in 1441, they captured a group of 12 African slaves. The Arabs, who so far had controlled the African slave trade, now had a rival.

In the 1480s, the Portuguese built a fort at Elmina on the west coast of Africa, in what is now Ghana. From here and similar places they would dominate the Atlantic slave trade when they and other Europeans began to look west, and explore the Americas. So began the next terrible stage in the history of slavery. Britain, and other European countries, later followed the Portuguese example and took slaves from West Africa.

## WHAT WAS AFRICA LIKE?

Some Africans were fishermen, hunters or gatherers, living in simple homes. Some were part of highly civilised societies such as the kingdom of Songhay which had a well-organised government, schools and a great city – Timbuktu. It is claimed that the university there had knowledge of eye surgery and even anaesthetics. In North Africa busy ports and market towns traded gold, ivory, crafts, skins, nuts and slaves. Traders came from as far away as India.

### NEW WORDS

**COLONIES:** land captured by another country abroad.
**ISLAM:** a religion started by the prophet Mohammed.
**KORAN:** the Sacred Book of Islam.
**NEW WORLD:** North and South America and nearby islands.
**PLANTATION:** an estate where crops are grown.

### SOURCE G

The kings of the Blacks sell their own people without justification.

▲ *Al Yaqubi, a 9th-century Arab geographer.*

### SOURCE H

▲ *The Portugese fort at Elmina.*

## SOURCE 1

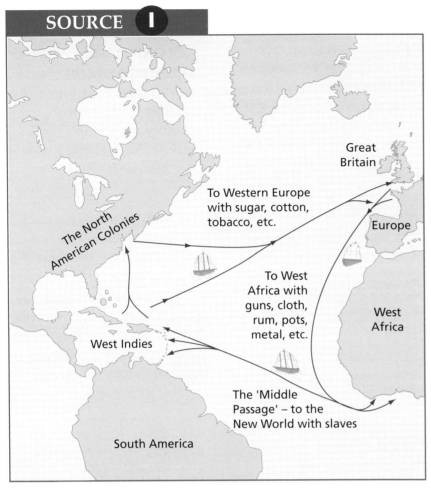

◄ *Map of how the 'triangular trade' worked.*

**Q** **1.** Why was there a need for slaves in the New World?

**2.** What was the difference between the slave system used by the Africans and slavery in America?

**3.** Explain the importance of the following in the story of African slavery:

- the Arabs
- African tribes and rulers
- West Coast African States
- the Portuguese
- the British.

## SLAVERY REACHES THE AMERICAS

From the late 15th century some European countries began to develop **colonies** in the Americas. They often fought each other to try to enlarge their colonies.

The Europeans faced very difficult conditions, such as extremely hot weather. They needed labour to build settlements and farm the land. Native Indians were used – but many caught diseases brought from Europe. In Central and South America, 18 million Indians died within a few decades. A stronger type of worker was apparently needed. Where were these workers to come from? The answer was obvious – Africa – where the Portuguese had by now a thriving slave trade. They soon began sending slaves to the Americas and by 1600, 80% were bound for this **New World**.

## SLAVERY AND PLANTATIONS

At first slaves were used in the Caribbean as well as Central and South America. They worked on **plantations** producing sugar, coffee, rice, cotton and tobacco. The British also decided to use slaves in their North American colonies, and the first group arrived at Jamestown, Virginia, in 1619.

Originally Black slaves were to be indentured servants (as some Whites were) who, if they worked hard, could be freed after a few years, and given land. For some slaves this was true, but in the southern part of Britain's colonies, the number of plantations grew, as farming became the main activity. More and more slaves were needed and a 'triangular trade' developed. These slaves, unlike slaves in Africa, were rarely freed. They lived and died as slaves.

In the late 1700s, however, the Colonies broke away from Britain, and the United States of America was formed. Northern areas abolished slavery, but in the South, where cotton was 'King', it became more important than ever.

# Slaves for the Americas

## CAPTURE

As we have already seen, African chiefs were willing to sell prisoners of war or even their own people in exchange for goods such as alcohol, cloth and jewellery. Charles Ball, a slave born in America, wrote a book about his life and described how he met some captives who had been brought from Africa. One of them told Ball how his village had been attacked by other Africans, who sold him to White men. This slave said he had never seen White people before and thought they were the ugliest creatures in the world! Some slaves were captured in an unusual way. One recalled how his grandmother had been taken prisoner when she followed a trail of red cloth dropped by White people. The slaves were kept at coastal trading ports where they were sold to White traders. They were then put on slave ships bound for America – to make the terrible journey known as the '**Middle Passage**'.

## NEW WORDS

**MIDDLE PASSAGE:** the sea voyage that was the second stage of the 'triangular trade'.
**SUPREME COURT:** the highest court in the USA.

*Diagram showing the way slaves were packed together on a slave ship, drawn in the late 18th century.* ▼

SOURCE Ⓐ

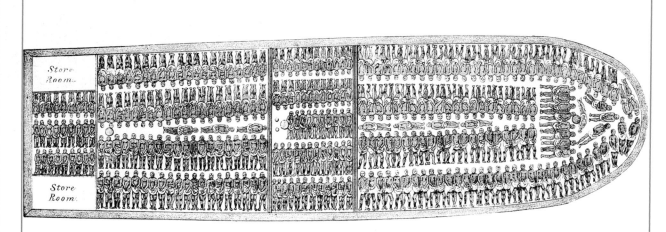

Store Room.

Store Room.

## VOYAGE TO AMERICA

If the weather in the Atlantic Ocean was bad: the voyage might take several weeks. Conditions on the ships were horrific. Terrified slaves, some of whom had never before seen the sea, were chained and packed into a small space. Angry slaves attacked members of the ship's crew. One sailor said slaves chained to the bottom deck tried to bite his ankles as he walked near them. Many were seasick and, at times, lay in their own vomit and waste.

Beatings were common but slaves who caused trouble or had a disease were thrown overboard to drown. Charles Ball was told by some newly arrived slaves that women with babies had their children taken from them as the slave ship left Africa. The babies were then thrown into the sea. Olaudah Equiano, who was captured at 11 years of age in the 1750s, described his voyage to the Americas when, like Charles Ball, he wrote his life story. He did not have enough room to turn around and was horrified by the screams of the women and the groans of the dying. Equiano eventually bought his freedom, set up a business in England and married a White woman.

If slaves tried to take over the ship they might be brutally killed. Very few uprisings succeeded. In 1839, however, slaves took over the *Amistad*. They demanded to be taken to Africa but the ship wound up in the USA. The slave owners went to court to get their slaves back. Eventually the **Supreme Court** became involved and the slaves were finally allowed to return to Africa in 1842. One of the men who defended the slaves was a former US President, John Quincy Adams. He made a speech on the slaves' behalf which lasted for more than eight hours!

▲ *Sick slaves thrown overboard (from a 19th-century picture).*

## SOURCE C

Two of the women leaped overboard after their children. The third was already confined by a chain but in the struggle to disengage [free] herself she broke her arm and died of fever.

▲ *Charles Ball, a slave who described what happened when three babies were thrown into the sea.*

 **1. Source A** was produced by an anti-slavery organisation. **Source C** is evidence provided by a slave. How valuable are these to historians trying to discover what life was like on the 'Middle Passage'?

**2.** Imagine you were a Black slave. Explain:

■ How you were captured.

■ Conditions on the slave ship.

■ How you felt about the White people who enslaved you.

# A 'Dark Continent'?

**YOUR MISSION: to discover what Africa was really like in the 18th century.**

In the 18th century many Europeans thought of Africa as the 'Dark Continent'. To them it was a mysterious place. Because they knew little about it, they often believed the strangest things. Worse than that, many White people looked down on Black people. They believed that Africans were not as civilised as White people. They believed that White people were superior. Look at the evidence in this Investigation and discover what a complex and amazing place Africa really was, and how skilled and clever its people were.

At least 12 million Black people were taken from Africa as slaves between 1532 and 1832. Some historians think that as many as 20 million Black people may have been captured.

Sahara

1

**1.** Bronze head made by a craftsperson of the Ife, a West African people.

**2. Central Africa.** *In the West rulers provided the Portugese with slaves. Further inland forest tribes had less contact with Whites but traded iron, copper, salt and ivory for European goods. Later they traded slaves too.*

**1. The Atlantic Coast.** *Explored by the Portugese since the 1470s. They traded European metal tools, jewellery and cloth for African gold and slaves captured in wars between different African peoples living inland in the forests.*

## INVESTIGATION

**You are the investigator!**
It is 1750 and you are compiling a report for the king of England on the real nature of Africa. In your report:

■ Mention how complicated its landscape is (with different kinds of areas ranging from grasslands to forests).

■ Mention the different kinds of African people and their different experiences of outsiders (Arabs and Europeans).

■ Describe the skills and crafts which show Black Africans to be a complex and clever people.

**1.** *Ivory salt cellar made in Benin, in West Africa.*

**5.** *The Nubian Christian cathedral at Dongola, turned into an Islamic mosque after Arab Islamic settlers pushed south.*

**5.** *The Ethiopian capital of Gondar.*

**5. North-eastern Africa.** *In Ethiopia the kingdom was Christian. Arab and Turkish traders brought Islam to other areas and traded for slaves.*

**4.** *The capital of the kingdom of Buganda in Central East Africa.*

**4. East Africa.** *Powerful kingdoms with little contact with Whites.*

Tropical rain forest

Tropical wood and grassland

Tropical grassland

Grass and thornbushes

Mountains and cool grassland

Desert and semi-desert

Mediterranean Forest and scrub

Coastal forests and scrubland

N

0          1000
kilometres

**3. Southern Africa.** *Small chiefdoms, cattle herders and hunters. Wars with Dutch settlers led to African land being seized by European settlers.*

**3.** *Khoisan herders setting up camp.*

# The auction block

**YOUR MISSION: to discover how slaves were sold in America**

After arriving in America, slaves were brought to **auctions** by slave traders, chained in what were called 'slave coffles'. Coffles were also used when slaves had been sold and were taken to their new homes. Those who were transported this way faced hardship and brutality. At the auction itself slaves were sold to the highest bidder. Some traders made a fortune. Nathan Bedford Forrest, who later became a general in the American **Civil War**, once made a profit of $96,000!

## FAMILIES DESTROYED

When the auction began, slave families were sometimes split up. Husbands and wives were separated as were brothers and sisters. Children were taken from their parents. On the day of the auction, people who were interested in buying slaves would be given an opportunity to examine them. Zamba, a slave who had arrived from Africa, said that when he was sold, White people would feel the limbs of the slaves in the same way that he had seen butchers examine cattle. Some slaves were fortunate enough to be sold to masters who treated them reasonably well but others would be bought by owners who had a reputation for cruelty. Every slave dreaded this. A few slave owners were in the business of breeding slaves for sale. Young healthy children would fetch a good price as a buyer could expect to get many years of work out of them.

## NEW WORDS

**AUCTION:** sale where articles are sold to the highest bidder.
**CIVIL WAR:** a war between different groups of people in the same country.

## SOURCE B

My mother told me that he [the master] owned a woman who was the mother of several children and when her babies would get a year or two of age he would sell them. When her fourth baby was born she said 'I'm not going to let the master sell this baby! She got up and give it something out of a bottle and pretty soon it was dead'.

▲ *Lou Smith, a Black slave in America.*

## SOURCE C

Massa have a great long whip and when one of the slaves falls behind or give out he hit them with his whip. Mother, she give out on the way. Her feet got raw and bleeding and her legs swoll plum out of shape. Massa just take out his gun and shot her and while she lay dying he kicks her. He just leave her laying where he shot her.

▲ *Ben Simpson, who was part of an early 19th-century slave coffle.*

## SOURCE A

▲ *A 19th-century slave auction in the USA.*

## SOURCE D

I said to him [a White buyer] 'For God's sake, have you bought my wife?' He said he had. He drew out a pistol and said that if I went near the wagon on which she was he would shoot me. I have never seen or heard from her from that day to this.

▲ *Moses Grandy, a slave.*

## SOURCE E

When I was 15 years old I was put up on the auction block to be sold. Old Judge Miller was there. He was so cruel that all of the slaves and many owners hated him. I told him 'Judge Miller! Don't you bid for me. I will take a knife and cut my own throat ear to ear before I would be owned by you.'

▲ *Delicia Patterson, a slave.*

## SOURCE F

My mother fell at the buyer's feet and clung to his knees begging him to buy her baby as well as herself. This man freed himself from her with violent blows and kicks.

▲ *Josiah Henson, a slave.*

One slave was bought by a wealthy man who set her free on the spot! This was, however, a very rare event.

## SOURCE G

They [the buyers] would stand the slave on the block and talk about what a fine looking specimen of Black manhood or womanhood they was – look in their mouth and examine their teeth just like they was a horse and talk about the kind of work they would be fit for.

▲ *Morris Hillyer, a slave.*

## SOURCE H

▲ *A slave being examined at a 19th-century US slave auction in the same way as a horse would be examined.*

## INVESTIGATION

**You are the investigator!**

Imagine that you are a slave. Write a conversation you might have with another slave telling how you have been sold. Here are the questions that they ask you. Write them down and your answers.

■ Why were you being sold?

■ How does the slave auction work?

■ How were you treated on your way to the auction?

■ What has happened to the rest of your family?

■ What do you feel about your future?

**11**

# 2 LIFE ON THE AMERICAN PLANTATIONS

## THIS CHAPTER ASKS
**What was the importance of cotton to the Southern states?**
**What was life like for slaves on the cotton plantations?**

### NEW WORDS

**RURAL:** to do with the countryside or farming.
**STATUS:** a person's rank or position in society.
**ECONOMY:** the ways in which a country earns its money.

## WHAT WAS THE IMPORTANCE OF COTTON?

Slaves brought to the Americas by the Europeans worked to produce a variety of crops, such as rice, tobacco, coffee and sugar. In the West Indies, for example, sugar dominated the economy, but as time passed, the Southern states of the USA concentrated on the production of cotton. The turning point came in the year 1793 when Eli Whitney invented a machine known as the cotton gin (engine). Before this, it could take a slave a full day to clean a small amount of cotton by hand.

One slave, West Turner, remembered how, after a long day working on the plantation, he and other slaves were required to clean a shoe-full of cotton before they were allowed to go to bed. Turner wore a size 14 shoe! Each night he was still cleaning his pile of cotton long after the rest of the slaves had finished. To stop this situation from getting worse, he wrapped his feet up very tightly in rags, to prevent them getting any bigger! Whitney's machine meant that slaves could clean 50 lbs (23 kg) of cotton per day. However, lots more slaves were still needed to pick the cotton. At the same time, demand for cotton greatly increased in Britain. There an 'Industrial Revolution' was taking place and steam power was being used in textile mills. Cotton was now big business. By 1861 cotton made up two thirds of all the United States' exports. The Southern states had a **rural economy** and cotton was crucial to their prosperity.

### SOURCE B

The wind, rain and snow blew in through the cracks and the floor was as miry as a pigsty.

▲ *Josiah Henson, a 19th-century slave describing his home. Miry means dirty.*

### SOURCE C

A small, square log cabin and a chimney made of sticks and mud.

▲ *Frederick Olmstead, describing the home of a poor White slave owner in the 1850s.*

### SOURCE D

The bed was a plank. My pillow was a stick of wood.

▲ *Solomon Northup, a 19th-century slave.*

### SOURCE A

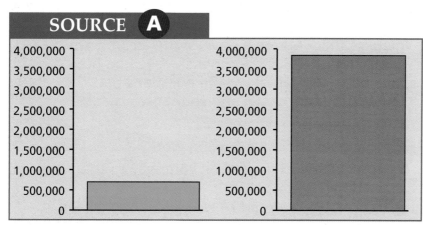

▲ **US Census 1790**
**Slave Population = 697,000**

**US Census 1860**
**Slave Population = 3,838,765**

## WHERE WAS COTTON GROWN?

The cotton crop was produced on plantations, which varied in size. About half of it was grown on small estates using less than six slaves. Some plantation owners were very rich and lived in huge mansions, often called the 'Big House'. But most lived in small houses. In fact some plantation owners lived in simple log cabins, and some were so poor they had to plough their own fields. Even the poorest White man, though, felt he should own at least one slave. This would give him more **status** than a man who did not own a slave. The slaves themselves lived in 'Slave Row' on the plantation. Their houses were poorly built. Many had mud floors and no windows. Often there was no furniture.

The slaves were made to work very hard. On larger plantations, overseers were hired to ensure they did their work. They were often very brutal. Some overseers were Black, and they were sometimes as brutal as the White overseers.

On cotton plantations the main work of the slaves was:

- planting the crop
- looking after the crop
- harvesting the crop.

After it was planted, the hoeing season (removing weeds) lasted from April to July. In August the cotton was picked. This was an incredibly busy time and slaves worked very long hours.

**Q**

**1.** Why did cotton play so important a part in American slavery? Mention:

- Eli Whitney
- Industrial Revolution
- US trade.

**2.** Using **Sources A–E**:

**a.** Describe the difference between the lifestyles of slaves and slave owners.

**b.** Why was the situation sometimes more complicated?

**Discussion Point:**
Why is 'status' so important to people? What kinds of things are used to give people status today?

**SOURCE E**

▲ *The 'Big House' on a large plantation.*

# What was life like on a plantation?

## WORK

Life was very hard on the cotton plantations. Slaves were given a production **quota** and in some places each one had to pick 200 lbs (91 kg) of cotton every day. The amount that had been picked was weighed and anyone who failed to meet their quota was punished. If they exceeded their quota, slaves were not rewarded. Instead they were given an even higher daily target. Slaves worked long hours, and in the picking season might have to labour through the night if the moonlight was good. Some were lucky enough to have jobs, which did not require them to work in the cotton fields. They were maids, cooks or butlers. Perhaps the best job to have was that of nanny to the master's children. To many of these children, their nanny was almost a second mother and a real bond of affection often existed.

Babies of field-workers might be looked after by elderly slaves. At times, however, mothers would have to bring their infants to the fields, and on one occasion this led to a terrible tragedy. An overseer told a group of women to leave their babies in a long wooden trough, near the place where they were working. Suddenly there was a heavy downpour. Within minutes the trough filled with water and all the babies drowned before their mothers could reach them.

## MUSIC AND CELEBRATIONS

Some owners allowed slaves to organise dances and, at Christmas, parties might be held. Music was very important to slaves. Slave songs often showed how they felt about their lives and they made music with whatever was available. One slave recalled how the horn of a buffalo was made into a flute.

Weddings were a cause for celebration. Some slaves were allowed to marry in the 'Big House' but many became man and wife by simply jumping over a broomstick! All slaves realised, however, that they were only married for as long as their master or mistress permitted it. He or she could sell them and split up families at any time.

## FOOD AND CLOTHING

Food was basic and the amount varied. If slaves had to be in the fields by dawn, their first meal might not be until midday. Clothes were often provided on a yearly basis but on some plantations, slaves worked virtually naked or in rags.

## NEW WORDS

**QUOTA:** a fixed amount.
**LYNCHED:** to judge and put to death without a trial.

## SOURCE A

The Massa's a good man an' I'll always try to please him

▲ *Charley Williams, a slave.*

## SOURCE B

The big bee flies high
The little bee makes the honey
Black folks make the cotton
And White folks get the money!

▲ *Part of a slave song.*

## REBELLIONS, ESCAPES AND PUNISHMENTS

Rebellions would be brutally crushed as the very idea of a slave revolt terrified the White slave-owners. They were horrified by the 1831 'Nat Turner Revolt' which killed nearly 60 White people. Turner was caught and hanged but Black people paid a terrible price for his revolt. Fifty-five of his followers were executed. A further 200 innocent Black people were **lynched**.

Some slaves resisted their masters in other ways. Some stole. Some destroyed crops and tools. Many ran away. A lot hid in woods and swamps. Others joined Indian tribes. One slave posted himself to the northern United States in a box.

*A slave being punished by a beating. A 19th-century ▼ American engraving.*

There Black people could live in freedom. He was later known as Henry 'Box' Brown.

Some runaway slaves were helped by a secret organisation run by White people in the northern states. This was called the 'Underground Railroad'. There was no actual railroad but railway terms were used as code words. So a 'station' was a house where runaway slaves could be hidden. One famous member of the 'Underground Railroad' was named Harriet Tubman. She acted as a guide. She was called the Moses of her people. This was because, like Moses in the Bible, she led her people out of slavery. She led some 300 slaves to freedom. Slave-owners offered $40,000 for her capture – dead, or alive!

Some slave-owners punished their slaves by burning them, or boiling them, alive.

**Q** Imagine you are a member of the 'Underground Railroad'.

Use the text and sources to write a speech designed to attract other slaves to join you.

Mention:

■ The worst aspects of plantation life.

■ Why the better parts of plantation life are still no substitute for freedom.

■ How the 'Railroad' works.

# 3 THE END OF SLAVERY IN THE AMERICAS

## THIS CHAPTER ASKS
**How did slavery end in the Americas?**
**Why was there a civil war in the USA?**
**What part did Blacks play in the Civil War?**
**Were Blacks really free in the USA after the Civil War?**

## NEW WORDS

**ABOLITIONISTS:** People in the Northern states who wanted to end slavery and formed a movement to achieve this.
**CONGRESS:** the law-making body or parliament of the USA.

During the 19th century, slavery was ended throughout the Americas. Great Britain, the world's strongest power, took the lead by ending slavery in her Caribbean colonies after pressure from people like the famous MP, William Wilberforce, and the Black leader, Equiano. The slave trade was ended by the British in 1807 and slavery was abolished in the British Empire in 1833. In the Americas, Black freedom fighters such as Toussaint L'Ouverture in Haiti, played a key role in the struggle to end slavery. In the USA, however, it would take a civil war to end slavery. Why did this war come about?

*The Northern view*

1. Why should you be able to produce things more cheaply than us by using slaves?

2. We want to protect our industries by taxing foreign goods to keep them out.

## CAUSES OF THE CIVIL WAR
For years people in the Northern and Southern states had argued about many things.

## THE SITUATION WORSENS
In the mid-1850s, there was violence in Kansas and Nebraska as the North and the South poured men and weapons into the area to decide whether it would be a 'free' or 'slave' state.
  The Dred Scott Case, in 1857, made things worse. Scott was a slave who had lived for years in parts of America where Black people were free. **Abolitionists** wanted him to be freed and the case reached the USA's highest court – the Supreme Court. Unfortunately the judge said that Scott had no right to be in a court as he was 'an ordinary article of merchandise' – and could be taken anywhere by his owner. Southerners now argued they had a right to take slaves to the new lands in the West. If this was the case, the balance between 'free' and 'slave' states in **Congress** would be lost. Northerners were furious.

3. New lands are opening up in the West and slaves must not be taken there. We do not want more 'slave' states than free states.

4. We don't like returning escaped slaves. Abolitionists say slavery is wrong! You should free the Black people. Harriet Beecher Stowe's book, Uncle Tom's Cabin, shows how cruel slavery is.

## SOURCE A

The Civil War

Map showing Union states, Confederate states, and Slave states that stayed in the Union, with Canada to the north and Mexico to the south. States labelled include Washington Terr., Oregon, Nevada, California, Utah Terr., New Mexico Terr., Nebraska Terr., Minnesota, Wisconsin, Michigan, Iowa, Illinois, Indiana, Ohio, Kansas, Missouri, Kentucky, Tennessee, Arkansas, Indian Terr., Texas, Louisiana, Mississippi, Alabama, Georgia, Florida, South Carolina, North Carolina, Virginia, WVA, Maryland, Delaware, New Jersey, Pennsylvania, New York, Connecticut, Rhode Island, Mass, Vermont, New Hampshire, Maine. Territories not yet states are marked.

0   200   400 miles

Key:
- Union states
- Confederate states
- Slave states that stayed in the Union

▲ **Map showing the sides in the American Civil War, 1861–5.**

*The Southern view*

1. You have industries – but we depend on farming. Cotton is vital and we need slaves to produce it. Your factory-workers are often low-paid and work in bad conditions. Isn't that a type of slavery?

2. Our cotton trade with other countries will suffer – if you tax their goods, they will tax ours.

3. If we agree to this you must accept the 'Fugitive Slaves Law' and return our escaped slaves.

4. Mrs Stowe and the Abolitionists are troublemakers! You Northerners should mind your own business!

## JOHN BROWN'S BODY LIES A MOULDERING IN THE GRAVE ...

Two years later, John Brown, a man who hated slavery, planned to invade the South to arm and free the slaves. During the earlier trouble in Kansas he had murdered five men because they believed in slavery. Brown was caught by the army and hanged, but his plan to arm the slaves frightened the South. As we have already seen, White Southerners were terrified of slave uprisings. To many Northerners, however, Brown was a hero. A famous song was written about him which claimed that while his body lay 'mouldering in the grave' , 'his soul goes marching on'. To those who supported him the fight against slavery would not stop until it was ended and Black people were free.

For the South, the final straw came in 1860 when Abraham Lincoln was elected President of the USA. He had spoken against slavery and did not want to see it in the new lands of the West. The South feared Lincoln would try to force them to end slavery. For them the issue was 'States' Rights' – the freedom of different states to decide their own laws without control by the central government. They decided to leave the USA and form their own country – the Confederate States of America. Lincoln said they could not leave. War began in 1861.

**Q**

**1.** Design two posters to be produced in 1861. Make one show the Northern view on slavery; one the Southern view.

**2.** Look at the 'arguments' and the other information on these pages. How far do you agree with the view that it was slavery that led to the American Civil War?

■ Show how arguments about slavery led to the war.

■ Show what other areas of disagreement existed.

**17**

# What did Black people do in the war?

## THE CIVIL WAR 1861–65

The war was a very bloody conflict fought between the Union army of the North, which was fighting to keep the USA together, and the Confederate forces of the South. Despite the courage of its army and the brilliance of its commander, Robert E. Lee, the South lost the war. Lee surrendered in April 1865.

## BLACKS IN THE NORTH

Many Black people wanted to join the Union army but some generals felt it was wrong to use them against White people. Others believed Blacks would make poor soldiers. By 1863, however, Northern casualties were heavy and the number of White volunteers had fallen. Black regiments were created and soon proved their fighting skills and courage in battle.

However, they were kept separate from White regiments and their soldiers received less pay than White recruits. They had Black officers, but their main commanders were White men such as Colonel Robert Gould Shaw, leader of the 54th Massachusetts Volunteers, who in 1864 charged a heavily defended Confederate base called Fort Wagner. Gould and half of his Black soldiers were killed. This action, however, earned the admiration of many Northerners. In the late-20th century the story of the attack was told in the Hollywood film, *Glory*.

Southerners were furious that Blacks were being used against them, and often murdered any they had captured. One of the worst atrocities occurred at Fort Pillow, near the Mississippi, where a large number of Black soldiers were murdered by Southern soldiers after they had surrendered.

## NEW WORDS

**DRAFT:** the system whereby men were called up to fight in the armed forces.

## SOURCE

The Northern army was more concerned about stealing than the freeing of poor slaves.

▲ *An anonymous slave commenting on the Civil War.*

## SOURCE

I'm fighting for $14 a month and the Union.

▲ *A Northern soldier's reply to a slave who said the North was fighting to end slavery.*

## SOURCE C

▲ *A Black Civil War regiment.*

About 179,000 Black soldiers served in the Union army and over 37,000 were killed. Black soldiers made up 12.5% of the Northern Army and 25% of the Northern navy. America's highest military decoration, the Congressional Medal of Honour, was introduced in the Civil War and 22 Black fighters received the award. Eventually their courage overcame racist attitudes in the North and they were paid the same wages as White soldiers.

Black people living in the North could not, however, be sure they were safe. When the number of White volunteers for the Union army fell, President Lincoln introduced 'the **draft**'. This was unpopular and many Whites, who felt the war was being fought for the benefit of Black people, turned against them. In cities like New York some Black people were shot down in the streets or lynched by mobs.

## BLACKS IN THE SOUTH

When Northern forces invaded, many slaves left the plantations and this led to a serious refugee problem. Some helped the Union army by building camps or doing other valuable work, such as aiding the wounded. Many Black people acted as guides or spies for the Union forces. One slave, Robert Smalls, together with some of his friends stole the Southern warship *Planter*, and handed it to the Union navy. Despite the help they gave the North, Southern Blacks were at times the victims of brutal treatment by racist Northern soldiers.

Some slaves, however, actually fought to defend the plantations against Union soldiers. At times they did this out of loyalty to their masters. Another reason was that they did not want to see the land ruined, which they hoped to gain a share of after the war.

**SOURCE** **D**

**Q**

**1.** Look at **Sources A** and **B**. How useful are these as evidence to an historian trying to decide why the North fought in the Civil War?

**2.** 'The 54th Massachusetts Volunteers were defeated at Fort Wagner but this was really a great victory for Black Americans.' Explain how this interpretation can be correct.

**3.** Explain the importance of the involvement of Black people in the American Civil War. Mention:

■ The length of the war and the need for soldiers.

■ The achievements of Black soldiers and sailors.

■ Help given to the North by Black civilians.

■ How Black achievements made them hope for better lives in the future.

The film character Forrest Gump was named after the Southern general, Nathan Bedford Forrest. He is still a hero in parts of the Southern states of America. But Forrest was a committed racist.

◄ *Northern racists in New York lynch a Black person in 1863.*

# A new dawn? (1865–1900)

SOURCE **A**

| | | |
|---|---|---|
| **1865** | 13th Amendment | Abolished slavery |
| **1868** | 14th Amendment | Blacks became US citizens protected by the law. |
| **1870** | 15th Amendment | Blacks could not be denied the right to vote. |

▲ *Changes in the Constitution of the USA.*

## NEW WORDS

**CONSTITUTION:** this lays down the rights of the people and the powers of the government.
**EMANCIPATION:** freedom.
**REPUBLICANS /DEMOCRATS:** America's two main political parties.
**SENATOR:** a member of the US Senate which along with Congress makes US laws.

### RECONSTRUCTION 1865–77

During the Civil War, President Lincoln's 1863 **Emancipation** Proclamation said the slaves were free – but actual freedom did not come until the war ended. Slavery was then finally abolished. Lincoln's government also created the Freedmen's Bureau to bring food and medicine to Whites and Blacks in a South devastated by war. It also set up schools for ex-slaves.

White Southerners, however, soon brought in the 'Black Codes'– laws to keep Black people on the plantations and to stop them moving around freely. President Lincoln died in 1865 and Congress was now controlled by members of the **Republican** party known as Radicals. Angered by the 'Black Codes', they wanted to punish the South and passed Reconstruction Acts which led to many Whites losing the right to vote. Black people, however, were gaining more rights – including the right to vote. Northern troops, including some Blacks, occupied the South to make sure Whites could not stop this.

Some ex-slaves became politicians in Southern state governments even though many could not even read or write. These governments, however, were controlled by 'carpetbaggers', who had moved south to make quick profits at the expense of a region crippled by war.

### WHITE SOUTHERNERS FIGHT BACK

Terrorist groups, such as the Ku Klux Klan, were formed. The Klan started as a social club for ex-Confederate soldiers; wearing their white robes, they realised they could terrify Black people. They would visit Black homes in the dead of night, pretending to be soldiers killed in the Civil War. One Klansman wore a false head, which he would remove. Nathan Bedford Forrest and others realised the Klan could be a powerful tool to keep Black people down. If they defied the Klan, Black people were beaten, lynched, burned, shot or drowned. Carpetbaggers, employees of the Freedman's Bureau and White Northern teachers, who helped to educate Blacks, were also threatened.

*Advances and Retreats in Black Rights after the Civil War.*

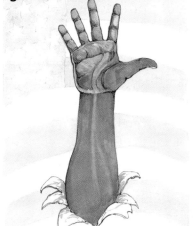

*'end of slavery', 'education', 'political rights'.*

*'Black Codes', 'Ku Klux Klan', 'Jim Crow laws of segregation'.*

## SOURCE B

Southern trees bear a strange fruit,
Blood on the leaves and blood at the root,
Black bodies swingin'
on the southern breeze,
Strange fruit hangin'
from the poplar trees …

▲ *An extract from a song by Billie Holliday.*

## SOURCE C

Smith was flogged and cut with knives. A heated iron was plunged down his throat. Spectators were invited to taunt and mutilate him further. The torture lasted for over two hours and then the platform was set alight. A recording was made of Smith's shrieks and a photographer took pictures. Both the record and these pictures could be bought in Texas for weeks after.

▲ *Death of a Black man, in Paris, Texas in 1893.*

# Q

**1.** Make a table with two columns.
Head one column: 'Changes for the better'. Head the other column: 'Changes for the worse'. Fill in each column with information about how life changed for Black people between 1865 and 1900.
**2.** Use your table to answer this question. How much did the lives of Black people improve after the Civil War?

## WHITE SOUTHERNERS REGAIN CONTROL

The Klan faded away when Northern troops finally left the South in 1877. A man called Rutherford B. Hayes had promised to remove them if the main political party in the South, the **Democrats**, backed him to be President of the USA. At the same time, Northern businessmen were keen to invest in the South and had their eyes not just on cotton, but a new industry – oil! As long as they could do business in the area Northerners were now willing to let Whites run the South once again. Soon the right to vote was taken away from Black people and Black politicians were sometimes physically thrown out of state government buildings. The 'Jim Crow' laws set up a system, which would exist in the South for decades – segregation. Black and White people were to be separated, eg Black children would not be allowed to attend the same schools as White youngsters. Blacks could not even sit on the same park benches as White people. In the 1890s a Black man called Homer Plessy took a railway company to court when he was told to leave part of a train where White passengers were sitting. The case reached the Supreme Court, and in the 1896 Plessy v Ferguson decision it ruled that separate facilities for Blacks and Whites were legal as long as those facilities were of an equal standard. This was the 'separate but equal' principle. Facilities for Black people, however, were rarely as good as those enjoyed by Whites!

## BRUTALITY RULES!

The system of segregation was enforced by brutality! Between 1882–1903, 2,000 Black people were lynched or burned. Southern newspapers would advertise these executions. Children would be taken to see them, as it was felt that lynchings were part of their education. One paper carried the headline: 'HARTFIELD [a Black man] WILL BE LYNCHED AT 5 O'CLOCK THIS AFTERNOON!' People often had their photos taken with the victims, knowing that no White person in the South would be convicted for the murder of a Black person.

The violence drove many Black people from the South before 1900. Some went to new lands in the West, while others tried to find work in northern cities, such as Chicago. This led to serious trouble as Northerners and others, including people who had emigrated to America, saw Black workers as competitors for jobs and housing.

**INVESTIGATION**

**YOUR MISSION: to find out whether the first half of the 20th century saw an an improvement in the position of Black people in the USA?**

## WHICH WAY FORWARD?

In the first half of the 20th century a number of different Black leaders emerged. Each had his own ideas about the way forward for Black people in the USA.

*BOOKER T. WASHINGTON*
**Background:**
*Founder of Tuskegee Institute – a training school for Blacks (1881)*
**Beliefs:**
*Blacks should learn skills in order to obtain decent jobs.*

*W.E.B. DU BOIS*
**Background:** .
*A graduate of Harvard University
A founder of **NAACP** (1909)*
**Beliefs:**
*Blacks should fight for full equal rights in every area of life.*

*MARCUS GARVEY*
**Background:**
*Founder of **UNIA**
1916 – moved to USA
1927 – Deported for alleged fraud*
**Beliefs:**
*Blacks should aim to set up a homeland in Africa.*

## SOURCE A

◄ **What does this advert for Pears soap say about White attitudes towards Blacks?**

## SOURCE B

The French Knew How To **WHITEN SKIN** Quickly-Safely-Surely

See How Sad

See How Happy

*After years of racism, some* ➤ *Blacks had a very poor image of themselves. Some desperately wanted to be White. They used chemicals to lighten the skin but this could lead to disfigurement, or even death.*

## HARD TIMES

Some Black people worked hard to set up businesses; others entered professions, such as law. There were outstanding success stories. Writer Claude McKay was popular with White readers; Louis Armstrong was a famous jazz musician while athlete Jesse Owens and boxer Joe Louis were sporting legends.

Black soldiers, who had fought for America, in World War One, however, returned to a country where Blacks were still victims of violence and often had the poorest housing and worst paid jobs. The situation worsened in 1929 when the US stock market crashed, putting millions of Americans out of work. Black workers, in particular, found it hard to get jobs.

## BLACK PEOPLE AND THE 'NEW DEAL'

In the 1930s President Franklin D. Roosevelt promised a 'New Deal' to get people back to work – but Blacks often failed to benefit. In the South a lot of Black people worked as 'sharecroppers'. White farmers gave them seed, tools and food and then took half of the crop they produced as well as the cost of these items. The result was that many Blacks were always in debt to the White farm owners and felt as though they were almost back in the days of slavery. Some fled at night to escape this.

## BLACKS IN WORLD WAR TWO

Blacks fought bravely in the war and many Black civilians did war work, such as making weapons. Even skilled workers, however, were often given the lowest paid jobs. Whites resented them and in the industrial northern city of Detroit in 1943, a riot left 25 Blacks dead.

## INVESTIGATION

**You are the investigator!**

1. Look at the ideas of the three Black leaders. In your opinion, which offered the best way forward?

2. 'Change' means things are different – and may be good or bad. 'Progress' involves improvement.

■ What things 'changed' for Black people between 1900 and 1945?

■ What 'progress' did Black people make in this period?

■ Do you think they made more progress between 1900–45 than between 1865–1900? Explain your answer.

### SOURCE C

WORLD'S HIGHEST STANDARD OF LIVING

There's no way like the American Way

◄ Photograph taken in the 1930s. Unemployed Black people queue for food in front of a poster advertising how wonderful life is in the USA. The people in the car are White.

### THIS CHAPTER ASKS

Why was segregation an important part of Southern life and how did Blacks come to challenge it?
What problems faced Blacks who challenged segregation?
Why and how was the Civil Rights Movement born?

## NEW WORDS

**DISCRIMINATION:** treatment in favour of – or against – a person, or group of people.
**DESEGREGATE:** mix, not separate.

### SEGREGATION

We have already seen how segregation was introduced in the Southern states. It could be seen at work in separate restaurants, waiting rooms, swimming pools and toilets. Segregation touched people in different ways. Mildred Taylor, a Black woman who lived in the North, remembers what happened when preparations were made for her to visit relatives in the South. Mildred's mother packed several baskets of food and filled a number of water jugs because her daughter would not be allowed to eat in Southern restaurants – or even drink at their water fountains.

Hospitals were also segregated. When Charles Drew, a doctor, was very badly injured in a car accident, he was turned away from a White hospital. Drew died before he could reach one which took Black patients.

| STATE | % of Negroes in population – 1963 | % of Negro in desegregated schools – 1963 |
| --- | --- | --- |
| Alabama | 30 | 0 |
| Arkansas | 21.8 | 0.25 |
| Florida | 17.8 | 0.55 |
| Georgia | 28.5 | 0.55 |
| Louisiana | 31.9 | 0.0362 |
| Mississippi | 42 | 9 |
| North Carolina | 24.5 | 0.3 |
| South Carolina | 34.8 | 0 |
| Tennessee | 16.6 | 0.9 |
| Texas | 12.4 | 2.17 |
| Virginia | 20.6 | 0.56 |

## SOURCE A

▲ *An example of the violence used to preserve White superiority.*

## SOURCE B

Listen. For a long time I had the idea that a man with White skin was superior because it appeared to me that he had everything, and I figured [that] if God would justify the White man having everything, that God had put him in a position to be the best.

▲ *Amzie Moore. As a Black person Amzie had almost come to believe the view of the world created by the racism of some Whites.*

### WHY WAS SEGREGATION CHALLENGED AFTER 1945?

At the end of World War Two many Blacks returned to America with a different outlook. They were determined to challenge poverty, **discrimination**, segregation and the terrible violence used to maintain these things. What had happened to make them feel this way?

Hundreds of thousands of Blacks had served in the US forces and saw parts of the world where they could mix with any race of people and where they were treated as ordinary human beings. In different parts of the world, non-White peoples were starting to gain freedom from White rule.

Some Blacks were inspired by outstanding success stories – Joe Louis was World Heavyweight Boxing Champion for twelve years, and Marian Anderson became the first Black person to sing a leading role in the New York Metropolitan Opera.

The National Association for the Advancement of Colored People (NAACP), set up in 1909. It now worked hard to achieve Civil Rights for all Black people. Civil Rights laws were eventually passed in 1957, 1960 and 1964. But it was hard to enforce these in Southern states.

The big breakthrough, however, came when the Supreme Court looked into the issue of segregation in schools. Interviews with Black children showed how this system had damaged them. Many actually felt that it was a bad thing to be Black. In 1954 the Supreme Court declared Black and White children should be allowed to attend the same schools. Most White Southerners were horrified. The Ku Klux Klan made a comeback and declared that the White race must be kept pure! In many Southern states the law to **desegregate** schools was ignored.

**Q**

**1.** Look at the Civil Rights spidergram. Which do you think is the most important Civil Right? Explain why. Can you think of any more Civil Rights which you would want to add to this diagram?

**2.** Design two spidergrams to show:
- Examples of segregation.
- The reasons some Blacks challenged it.

**3.** To what extent had segregation been challenged by the end of the 1960s?
- Think about what had existed in 1945.
- Think about what had been challenged.
- Think about what remained to be done.

The right to be protected by the law.

The right to participate in government.

The right to vote in elections.

CIVIL RIGHTS

The right to have equal access to amenities (eg shops, restaurants).

The right to equal health care and education.

# Problems on the 'road' to Civil Rights

## SOURCE A

▲ Getting water by hand.

## SOURCE B

▲ Black homes sharing an outdoor toilet.

## SOURCE C

◄ Run-down Black school with poor equipment.

The cost of keeping two school systems going in Southern states (one for Whites/one for Blacks) was so expensive that neither system could work properly.

## SOURCE D

WAITING ROOM
FOR WHITE ONLY
→
BY ORDER
POLICE DEPT.

▲ Segregated waiting room.

## SOURCE E

▲ White women protesting against a Black Civil Rights march.

## SOURCE F

◄ *White racist demonstration.*

## SOURCE G

▲ *Ku Klux Klan sign outside a Southern town.*

## SOURCE H

▲ *Ku Klux Klan members with their small child.*

## SOURCE I

▲ *Southern police officers use sticks to break up a Black protest march.*

## SOURCE J

▲ *White youths protesting at Black children coming to their school.*

**Q**

**1. a.** Make a list of things Black people were struggling to change;

**b.** make a list of the problems that were facing them.

**2.** How useful are photographs like these as evidence for the problems faced by Black people in the early 1960s?

**27**

# The murder of Emmett Till

**YOUR MISSION: to discover what effect the murder of Emmett Till had on the determination of Black people to end segregation and achieve civil rights**

## NEW WORDS

**TESTIMONY:** evidence given by a witness.

## EMMETT'S STORY

This story takes place in Mississippi, which had more Black people in its population than any other state. Indeed, if you were Black, it could be a very dangerous place! Several hundred Black people had been lynched since the end of the Civil War.

In the segregated South, Black boys did not have White girlfriends. If a Black man even stared at a White woman he might suffer terrible violence. Emmett Till, a 14-year-old boy from Chicago in the North, had not understood this and paid for this with his life.

In 1955, Till was visiting his great-uncle, Mose Wright, who lived on a farm near the Mississippi town of Money. One day, he was talking to some local Black boys outside a store run by the Bryant family. Till had photographs of his Chicago school friends. Some were White, and Till even said that he had a White girlfriend. The other boys found this hard to believe, because in Mississippi such things were not allowed. They dared Till to start a conversation with the White woman serving in the store. Till took up the challenge.

## TALKING TO A WHITE WOMAN

We cannot be sure what was said, but the Chicago boy's cousin thought Till had used the words 'Bye, baby!' when he left the store. The woman was the wife of the storeowner, Roy Bryant. She told her husband that she had been spoken to in a way which had not shown respect. He decided to act.

## MURDER

Several days later, at 2.30 am, Roy Bryant and a man called J.W. Milam took Till away from Mose Wright's farm. He was never seen alive again. The boy was brutally murdered, tied to part of a cotton gin with barbed wire and dumped in the Tallahatchie River. However, the body floated to the surface. It was in a horribly mutilated state and could only be identified by a ring, which had Till's initials on it.

## SOURCE A

Sunday mornin' about 2.30 someone called at the door … and he said 'This is Mr Bryant' … And when I opened the door, there was a man standing with a pistol in one hand and a flashlight in the other hand … And he said, '…I wants the boy that done all that talk.' And they marched him [Emmett Till] to the car …

▲ *Mose Wright, great-uncle of Emmett Till.*

## SOURCE B

▲ *Emmett Till.*

## THE TRIAL

Bryant and Milam were arrested and put on trial. Mose Wright was the key witness, as he had seen these men take his nephew away. The Ku Klux Klan threatened Wright's life and he was forced to go into hiding until the trial. The NAACP played a key role at this time. They helped to protect Mose Wright and also ensured that the trial received publicity. When he was called to give evidence Wright stood up in the courtroom to identify the man who had taken his young relative. He pointed to Roy Bryant. Despite Wright's **testimony** and those of other witnesses, Bryant and Milam were found not guilty by an all-White jury, who took one hour to reach this verdict. Someone claimed it only took that long because they had stopped to drink a coke!

## AFTER THE TRIAL

Some months later, Bryant and Milam sold their story to a newspaper reporter, William Bradford Huie, for $4000. Huie said that Milam had been angered about two things when he and Bryant took Till away. They expected him to be both frightened and sorry for what he had said to Mrs Bryant. The boy, however, had shown no fear. Nor did he apologise. Secondly, Till had told them about his White girlfriend. From that moment on he was going to die.

Bryant and Milam got away with murder and even made money from their crime. The brave challenges of Mose Wright and other witnesses had failed to get justice in the courts – but Till's story made other Black people even more determined to end the unfair treatment of Blacks in the South. They now looked for a victory.

## SOURCE C

There was no expectation that White people who murdered Negroes [in Mississippi] would ever be brought to justice.

▲ *Myrlie Evers, wife of Medgar Evers – an NAACP leader.*

## SOURCE D

The whole trial was just a farce.

▲ *Mamie Till Bradley.*

## SOURCE E

When he told me about the White girl he has, I looked at him and said, 'Boy – you ain't gonna never see the sun come up again.'

▲ *Milam speaking to W.B. Huie.*

## INVESTIGATION

### You are the investigator!

It is 1955 and you are a British journalist covering the Emmett Till case. Write an article for your newspaper back home. In it:

■ Describe who Emmett Till was.

■ Explain why it is believed that this crime happened.

■ Write 'eyewitness' accounts by Bryant and Milam in which they explain why they killed Emmett.

■ Explain why the verdict in this case has shocked so many people and why it may lead to changes in the way Black people are treated.

# Rosa Parks and the Bus Boycott

**YOUR MISSION: to find out how the story of Rosa Parks helped to create an organised Civil Rights Movement.**

## NEW WORDS

**BOYCOTT:** to refuse to take part in something, or buy a product or service, as a way of making a protest.
**SCLC:** Southern Christian Leadership Conference.

## ROSA'S STORY

In the 1950s Montgomery, Alabama, was a major centre for cotton, timber and livestock, but many Black workers were poor and had low-paid jobs. A number of Black women, for example, worked as maids for White families. The buses were segregated. White passengers sat in the front, while Black passengers occupied the back. They could, however, take a seat in the middle rows if no White person was already sitting there.

In December 1955, Rosa Parks was travelling home after a long day's work. She sat down in the middle row of the bus. Soon it filled with passengers. A White man found that he had no seat. The driver told the Black people in the middle rows to give up their seats and most of them did. Rosa Parks, however, refused. A police officer was called by the driver and she was arrested, fingerprinted, jailed and fined.

The NAACP in Montgomery was very angry and wanted Black people to **boycott** the buses. They asked a newly arrived clergyman, Martin Luther King, to lead this boycott. King agreed. He was a highly educated man who believed in the idea of non-violent protest, which had been used by Mahatma Gandhi during India's struggle to gain independence from Great Britain. King often kept the determination of the boycotters going by his rousing speeches.

## SOURCE A

The four of us [in the middle row] would have to stand up for this one White passenger. The driver asked if I was going to stand up. I told him no. He said, 'I'm going to have you arrested.' The policeman asked, 'Why didn't you stand up?' I said, ' I didn't think I should have to. Why do you push us around?' He said, 'I don't know – but the law is the law, and you are under arrest'

▲ *Rosa Parks describes her arrest.*

## SOURCE B

▲ *Rosa Parks being fingerprinted for her 'crime'.*

## SOURCE C

We are tired of going through the long night of captivity and now we are reaching out for the daybreak of freedom, justice and equality ... In our protest, there will be no cross burnings. No White person will be taken from his home by a hooded Negro mob and brutally murdered. If you protest with dignity and Christian love, the historians will say – there lived a great people.

▲ *Martin Luther King speaking during the Bus Boycott.*

## THE BOYCOTT, DECEMBER 1955–DECEMBER 1956

Thousands of notices were sent to Black people to persuade them to join the boycott. A local newspaper unintentionally helped by carrying a front-page story warning Whites of the boycott. In fact it helped to spread the word to even more Blacks. The boycott would last for just over a year, and in the meantime many Blacks suffered at the hands of some of the more aggressive Whites.

Police threatened to take away the driving licence of any Black driver who gave lifts to boycotters. Those who were caught waiting for lifts were sometimes arrested for loitering! Gangs of Whites often beat up Blacks in the streets and the police did nothing to help. Martin Luther King, whose leadership had kept the boycott going, was arrested, but worse was to follow. His house was bombed. There were even times when Black churches were blown up.

In November 1956, the Supreme Court said segregation on buses was wrong. The boycotters had won! The bus companies were relieved that the protest was over. As most bus passengers were Black, the companies had lost a great deal of money. This victory in Mongomery led to other boycotts in the South.

From December 1955 to December 1956, the eyes, not only of America, but also of other nations in the World were focused on Montgomery. King became famous in his own country and abroad. The action taken here was the start of a Civil Rights Movement he helped to create. From 1957 his **SCLC** group would fight segregation wherever they found it in the South.

# INVESTIGATION

**You are the investigator!**

Imagine you were with Rosa Parks when she was arrested.

■ Explain why she refused to move.

■ Describe how she was treated.

■ Describe how the boycott followed this, and how Martin Luther King became a Black Civil Rights leader through it.

■ Decide why Rosa Parks got justice when Emmett Till did not.

A Black man was filling his car with petrol when a White woman demanded he step aside to let her use the pump. When he refused a White mob chased him, tied him to the back of a vehicle and dragged him along until he was dead.

## SOURCE D

◄ Rosa Parks sits at the front of a bus in 1956, after segregation on public transport was banned.

> **THIS CHAPTER ASKS**
> What barriers faced Black people fighting for civil rights 1951–1965?
> What kind of challenges were made and how successful were they?

In Chapter 4 we learned how, in the 1950s, an organised Civil Rights movement was born. It aimed to end segregation. It also wanted to win voting rights for all Black people. There would be no single 'battlefield' in the struggle, however; the conflict would be fought in several different areas of everyday life in the South.

## THE RIGHTS BEING 'FOUGHT' FOR

In education Black people wanted the right to attend good, all-White schools and universities. They wanted to be able to use the same public facilities as White people – such as lunch counters in the large department stores. Inter-state buses were still not desegregated. They wanted to change this. As we saw earlier, Southern Blacks did not have voting rights for very long. The Civil Rights Movement wanted them **restored**. While 'fighting' to bring about these changes, however, there would also be a battle for people's hearts and minds. Martin Luther King hoped the method of non-violent protest would win support for their cause by showing that Black people could behave with dignity – even when facing White brutality.

## THE DIFFICULTIES ENCOUNTERED

Many White Southerners did not want to see the changes that King's movement and other Civil Rights protesters were aiming for. At every step, therefore, they faced fierce resistance. As well as groups such as the Klan, White Citizens' Councils were set up. Their members included business people, lawyers, teachers, doctors, clergymen and others. These groups did not wear white hoods. They operated in a different way. In 1955, when a group of Black people in Orangeburg, South Carolina, wanted their children to attend a White school, the local Citizens' Council got to work. Nearly every Black person who had a White employer was sacked. Blacks who rented homes from Whites were **evicted** and some White businesses would not sell goods to Black people. The Councils **influenced** politicians and often used newspaper adverts to spread their ideas. If it was felt to be necessary, however, the White Citizens' Councils would also use violence.

### NEW WORDS

**DIXIE:** the Southern states of the USA.
**EVICTED:** thrown out of a place.
**FBI:** the police with responsibility for Federal Laws which apply in every state of the USA.
**INFLUENCED:** had an effect on a person or idea.
**RESTORED:** given back.

### SOURCE A

All the people of the South are in favour of segregation and Supreme Court, or no Supreme Court, we are going to maintain segregated schools down in **Dixie**.

▲ *Senator James Eastland of Mississippi.*

### SOURCE B

The people of the South have always fed folk who asked for something to eat. They have also reserved the right to eat only with invited guests.

▲ *A White Southerner.*

### THE POLICE
The police also presented a problem for the Civil Rights Movement. In the South local officers might be members of the Klan or White Citizens' Councils.

### THE FBI
For a long time even the Federal Bureau of Investigation (**FBI**) did little to help Black people. Their chief, J. Edgar Hoover, did not like the Klan, but he also saw Martin Luther King as a dangerous threat – someone who was using the Civil Rights Movement to cause trouble on the streets of America. Another reason the FBI did little to help Blacks was that sometimes their agents needed the help of the local state police forces and they did not want to take action which would lose them this co-operation. The Bureau also felt all-White juries were never going to convict a White man of the murder of a Black person.

### STATE GOVERNORS
Southern governors also were against the Civil Rights Movement. They saw it as their responsibility to protect the Southern way of life. They wanted things to remain the same. This meant protecting segregation.

**Problems facing the Civil Rights Movement.**

Inactive FBI.

Ku Klux Klan.

Racists in the Southern police.

White Citizens' Councils.

Many Southern politicians.

### SOURCE C
Desegregation is against the Bible.

▲ *A claim made by Reverend William Carter.*

### SOURCE D
… no school in our state will be integrated while I am your governor. I now call on every … citizen … to join with me in refusing … to submit.

▲ *Ross Barnett, Governor of Mississippi.*

### SOURCE E
Segregation now, segregation tomorrow and segregation forever.

▲ *George Wallace, Governor of Alabama.*

On 28 August 1963, the largest demonstration that Washington had ever seen brought over 200,000 Black and White people onto the streets calling for 'Jobs and Freedom'.

**Q**

**1.** Segregation was not just enforced by terrorists, it was seen as part of Southern life and the law. Can you find evidence for this?

**2.** Explain the problems facing the Civil Rights Movement from:
■ White Citizens' Councils
■ the police
■ the FBI
■ State governors.

Say how each one made their job more difficult.

# How far did the 'challengers' succeeed?

The Black people challenging White power in the 1950s and 60s did so in a number of areas. But how succesful were they?

THINKING IT THROUGH

## EDUCATION

In 1954 the US Supreme Court declared segregated schools were wrong. It is, however, one thing to pass a law – but another to get people to accept it. This can be difficult. A key test came at Little Rock, Arkansas, in 1957. Nine very able Black students were allowed to attend what had always been an all-White high school. On the first day, one Black student, Elizabeth Eckford, arrived at the school alone. A mob of angry Whites surrounded her and some even threatened to kill her. However, local police and soldiers of the state National Guard did nothing to help her – she was 'rescued' by a local White woman, who put her on a bus.

Three days later President Dwight Eisenhower sent paratroops to Little Rock and the nine young people were taken to school by an armed escort every day. Soldiers even took the students to each class. After a year the state governor closed the school. Some other state governors did the same to stop desegregation.

## HIGHER EDUCATION

James Meredith, a Black student, wished to attend the University of Mississippi. There was only one problem – the university was for Whites only. When he finally did win the right to a place in 1962, the Governor of Mississippi himself, Ross Barnett, stopped him from entering the building. America's president had to send 500 US marshals to the university. Meredith took his place – but it led to a riot – and two people died before order was restored.

## PUBLIC FACILITIES: THE LUNCH COUNTER SIT-INS, 1960

Although Black Americans in the South could buy goods in the department stores they were not allowed to use the lunch counters. In 1960, in Nashville, Tennessee, Black students who were part of **SNCC** decided to challenge this. They selected a number of stores and sat at the lunch counters. The staff refused to serve them, but they continued to occupy seats at the counters every day. At first, they were sworn at and had ketchup, salt and other things things poured on them.

### NEW WORDS

**ATTORNEY GENERAL:** person in the government in charge of the law.
**CORE:** Congress of Racial Equality.
**SNCC:** Student Non-Violent Co-ordinating Committee, a group which believed in the ideas of Martin Luther King.

Special training helped the young students in the sit-ins to remain calm and not to react in anger when they were yelled at, humiliated and even dragged from their stools.

SOURCE **A**

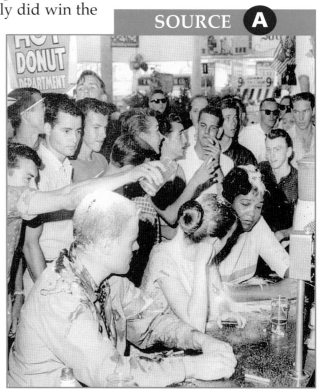

▲ *A lunch counter sit-in.*

## WHITE VIOLENCE. BLACKS ARRESTED!

One day a White mob attacked and savagely beat a number of lunch counter protesters. Police ignored this. They waited until the mob had done its work – then arrested their Black victims! This pattern was repeated as more students came to sit at the counters. Ordinary Black citizens now decided to boycott the stores and even White customers stayed away because they feared violence. The store owners, of course, were losing a lot of money. Eventually, however, the lunch counters were opened to Blacks as well as Whites. Sit-ins in other cities were also successful.

## TRANSPORT

In 1960 the Supreme Court said there should be no segregation on buses travelling between states, (eg Greyhound buses). **CORE**, a Civil Rights group founded in the 1940s, wanted to put this decision to the test. They wanted to know whether it would be enforced if Black and White passengers sitting on a bus together met opposition when they travelled from the North to the South. The new president, John F. Kennedy, seemed to favour Black Civil Rights – but he acted in a cautious way. It appeared he might need Southern votes to be re-elected. To CORE he seemed to be dragging his feet, so they took action! In 1961 two buses of Black and White passengers, called 'freedom riders', left Washington DC to travel through the South to New Orleans.

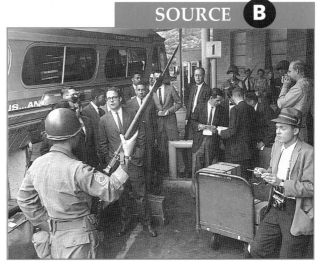

SOURCE **B**

▲ *Freedom riders of Montgomery, Alabama, needed armed guards for protection.*

## VIOLENCE

One bus was fire-bombed at Anniston, Alabama, and Whites tried to block the exits. The second bus was met by a mob in Birmingham. SNCC students joined the bus to keep the ride alive but they encountered a another mob at Montgomery. White 'freedom riders' were particularly savagely beaten.

Alabama's governor, John Patterson, would give no protection, nor did the FBI. America's **Attorney General**, Robert Kennedy (brother of the President), did try to help, however. US marshals were sent to the area – but were too late! So what was the outcome? The riders did not reach their destination, New Orleans, but Robert Kennedy did enforce the ban on segregation on inter-state transport.

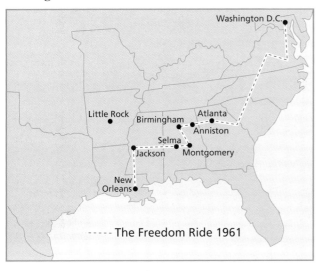

----- The Freedom Ride 1961

**Q**

**1.** Look at these areas of life: Education, Public facilities, Transport. For each, explain problems facing Black people. Describe how they challenged the problems. Decide how successful you think that they were.

**2.** What questions would you ask about **Sources A** and **B**, to judge how useful they were for deciding how Black People were treated across the Southern states?

## POLITICS

To Martin Luther King, Birmingham was the South's most segregated city. Frequent attacks on Black homes and churches earned it the nickname 'Bombingham'. Blacks had few job opportunities and could not vote. Police Commissioner, 'Bull' Connor, saw that segregation was enforced. King organised boycotts, sit-ins and tried to help Black people register for the right to vote. Police used tear gas, electric cattle prods and batons – even against school children who had answered King's call to help. Dogs were used to tear into the protesters while the Fire Department used hoses against them. A Black church was bombed, killing four young schoolgirls. There were, however, many White people in Birmingham, including local leaders, who were sickened by the violence. They said it must not be allowed to go on. This, action by local leaders is what brought about the end of segregation in their city in 1963.

## THE POLICE

Local police would remain a problem, but President Johnson, who replaced the murdered President Kennedy in 1963, wanted the FBI to become tougher in the fight against groups such as the Klan who targeted not only Black people, but also White people who supported them. These were referred to as 'nigger lovers'. In Mississippi, in 1964 three young Civil Rights workers from the North, Michael Schwerner, James Chaney and Andrew Goodman, vanished. The FBI launched a massive investigation and found their bodies. They had been murdered. Not until 1997 was a member of the Ku Klux Klan – Henry Hayes – executed for the murder of a Black person.

## HEARTS AND MINDS

King's method of non-violent protest won admiration in America and abroad, and Black people by their dignity, even when facing terrible violence, had won great support. 250,000 people flocked to hear King speak in Washington in 1963. The FBI, however, continued to view King as an enemy of America. It was so suspicious of him, that it 'bugged' his phone and his home. Nevertheless, in 1964, he was given one of the world's highest awards – the Nobel Peace Prize.

**SOURCE C**

▲ *Martin Luther King, addressing the crowd at the 1963 Washington Rally.*

**SOURCE D**

▲ *Methods used to crush protest.*

## SOURCE E

If an American, because his skin is dark, cannot eat lunch in a restaurant open to the public; if he cannot send his children to the best school available, if he cannot vote – if he cannot enjoy the full and free life which all of us want, then who among us would have the colour of his skin changed and stand in his place?

▲ *President Kennedy, speaking on nationwide television.*

## SOURCE F

| Percentage of Black People in population | % of these Black People entitled to vote |
|---|---|
| Alabama 30 | 13.7 |
| Arkansas 21.8 | 37.7 |
| Florida 17.8 | 39 |
| Georgia 28.5 | 28.4 |
| Lousiana 31.9 | 30.9 |
| Mississippi 42 | 6.1 |
| N. Carolina 24.5 | 38.2 |
| S. Carolina 34.8 | 4.7 |
| Tennessee 16.5 | 64 |
| Texas 12.4 | 33 |
| Virginia 20.6 | 23 |

▲ *Black people in the South,1962.*

## VOTING RIGHTS

In the early 1960s many Blacks in areas of the South could not vote. Before their names could go on the voters' register they had to pass a test. These tests were 'fixed' so that it was very difficult for a Black person to pass. Then there was the threat of violence.

After events in Birmingham, President Kennedy wanted a new Civil Rights act. In a world where Communist countries, such as Russia and China, did not allow their people basic freedoms, he knew that America saw itself as the champion of democracy and human rights. Yet it was denying basic rights to its Black citizens. This new act, then, was to protect the Black right to vote and ban discrimination and segregation for good. It became law in 1964 but Southern states still tried to stop Black people voting. Kennedy did not live to see the law passed. He was assassinated in 1963.

## ANOTHER STEP FORWARD

A non-violent protest march was organised in 1965. Marchers would walk from Selma to Montgomery to protest about the lack of voting rights. The police attacked the marchers at a place called Pettus Bridge. Tear gas and clubs were used whilst mounted police ran some of the marchers down. Television captured these images. The American public was shocked. King had not been able to attend the first march but came for a second one which was given army protection. President Johnson had ordered this protection and, in 1965, he made sure Black voting rights were guaranteed by law.

## SOURCE G

I have a dream that my four little children will one day live in a nation where they will not be judged by the colour of their skin – but by their character.

*Martin Luther King, speaking at the Washington Rally, in 1963.*

**Q**

**1.** Why was getting the vote such an important step forward for Black people?

**2.** Look at **Source E**. Why was this speech a 'turning point' in the struggle for Black Civil Rights?

**3.** Imagine you are a member of the Nobel Peace Prize selection panel. Write a report on the work of Martin Luther King explaining why he should get a prize for working for peace. Look at all the information on him in this book so far. Use the index to help you.

# A Mississippi murder

**YOUR MISSION: to discover whether it was possible for a Black person to obtain justice in Mississippi.**

*Witness: Police called to the scene of the crime*

In Mississippi law and terror kept Whites in control. No US state had such a terrible record of violence against Blacks and no White man had ever been convicted of killing one.

*Witness: A Black neighbour.*

Medgar Evers had seen Blacks being beaten. Many even had to ask for permission before they could go into town. Black people who dared consider registering to vote were threatened. Evers joined the NAACP. When Emmett Till was killed in 1955, Evers investigated the case and helped to gather witnesses. Later Evers led a campaign to help register Black people to vote. In the year he was murdered he organised a boycott of White stores.

*Witness: A member of the NAACP.*

In June 1963 we were called to the home of Medgar Evers in Jackson, Mississippi. We found he had been shot in the back, outside his home. The bullet which had hit and had killed him, smashed through the living room and the kitchen where it made a dent in the fridge. He was at the top of a Ku Klux Klan hit list.

*Witness: Mrs Myrlie Evers.*

Destroy the enemy! [Referring to Black Civil Rights workers.]

*Witness: Byron de la Beckwith. Accused of the crime*

To keep his family safe, my husband, Medgar, told us, 'Stay away from lighted windows. If you hear any strange noise – get down on the floor'.

God put us here to rule over the dusky races ... [we must be prepared for] the extermination of all who oppose us.

*Witness: Ross Barnett, Governor of Mississippi, 1960–4.*

*Witness: A white friend of Beckwith.*

The murder weapon was traced to Byron de la Beckwith and a storekeeper confirmed that he had sold Beckwith a telescopic sight for the gun.

I saw Byron 90 miles away when the murder took place. He was filling his car with petrol at the time.

*Witness: The Prosecution lawyer.*

Beckwith asked me if I knew Evers and the area he lived in.

*Witness: Herbert Speight, Taxi driver.*

We saw Beckwith near Evers's home.

*Witness: Bystanders.*

The bullet which hit Medgar Evers in the back and killed him cannot definitely be traced to the gun which bore Beckwith's fingerprint because it was so badly damaged.

Beckwith was ninety miles away at the time of the killing.

*Witness: The Defence lawyer.*

*Witness: Two policemen. Both members of a White Citizens' Council.*

A fingerprint on the murder weapon matched that of Beckwith's right index finger.

*Witness: Ralph Hargrove, Fingerprint expert.*

At the end of the trial the all-White jury could not reach a verdict. A second trial ended in the same way. Beckwith walked free! But Myrlie Evers wanted Beckwith brought to justice. In 1994 he was tried again – and sentenced to life imprisonment.

*Witness: Newspaper reporter*

# INVESTIGATION

## You are the investigator!

You are the lawyer prosecuting Beckwith. Write the speech you will give to the jury.

■ Note the evidence linking him to the crime. Say why you think it is strong evidence.

■ Go through evidence in Beckwith's defence and say why you do not think it clears him.

■ Sum up by saying what you think was Beckwith's motive. Mention anyone else you think shares some responsibility for the killing.

## THIS CHAPTER ASKS
Why did some Black people turn away from non-violence in the 1960s?
What were the beliefs of Black militant groups?
To what extent has the position of Black Americans improved?

## NEW WORDS
**MILITANT:** prepared to fight, or be aggressive in some other way, to further a cause.
**SLUM:** poor area with bad housing.

## DISILLUSIONMENT
Despite the successes of the Civil Rights Movement, and the non-violent tactics of Martin Luther King, many Black people in the mid 1960s felt very angry and there was a great deal of unrest. Why was this the case?

Many Black people lived in the **slum** areas of America's cities and had to put up with poor housing, as well as the worst paid jobs. The Black unemployment rate was twice as high as that for White people. Black people also felt they were often the victims of police brutality.

In 1965, when Annie Lee Cooper, a Black woman, tried to vote in Alabama, the local White sheriff smashed her over the head with a club.

### SOURCE A

▲ A Black home in the 1960s.

### SOURCE B

▲ A Black home in the 1880s.

**SOURCE C**

▲ *Watts, Los Angeles after the riots, August 1965.*

**SOURCE D**

▲ *Smith and Carlos at the 1968 Olympics.*

## MILITANT ACTION

Many Black people felt that peaceful protests were simply not working and some turned away from non-violent ideas. They looked to **militant** groups, such as the Black Muslims, Black Panthers and the Black Power movement. Black anger also showed itself in the form of riots, which took place in 25 cities across America between 1964 and 1967. Nearly 150 people were killed and more than 4,500 injured. In the Watts area of Los Angeles, where the Black unemployment rate was three times higher than the national rate for White people, a riot in 1965 left 34 people dead, 1,000 injured and 200 buildings destroyed.

## DRAMA AT THE OLYMPICS

Millions of television viewers watching the 1968 Olympic Games saw two Black athletes, Tommie Smith and John Carlos, receive their medals for the 200m event and then bow their heads and give the Black Power salute as the American national anthem was played. The athletes were sent home in disgrace as it was felt they had insulted their flag and country. Smith and Carlos were never allowed to compete for America again, and for years both men struggled to find jobs.

## KNOWLEDGE IS POWER

Black parents wanted a better existence, not only for themselves but also for their children. How were they to achieve this? Many thought the answer lay in improving Black education. It was realised that to compete with young White people for better paid jobs, Black students needed to study for higher qualifications. Many Black people therefore demanded more university places for Black students. It was also felt that colleges should have more Black lecturers. There was also a feeling that Black people should know more about their own past and traditions. As a result, there were calls for colleges to provide courses in Black history and culture.

**Q**

**1.** Look at **Sources A** and **B**. Describe each home. What does this suggest about improvements in Black living conditions between 1880 and 1965?

**2.** Why did some Black people turn away from the idea of non-violence?

**3.** List the actions taken by militant Black people and say if, in your opinion, each one helped or damaged the Civil Rights Movement.

# Different paths to freedom?

Martin Luther King was assassinated in 1968. In the years before his murder, he saw the Civil Rights Movement change. It split as new – militant – groups grew up. We need to ask:

1. Who were these groups?
2. Who were their leaders, and what did they believe?
3. How did their ideas differ from those of Martin Luther King?

## NEW WORDS

**BLACK SEPARATISM:** Black people should live in their own areas and have a separate government from White Americans.

> Black and White people should not live together. We Blacks should have our own part of America and, if necessary, we must fight the White devils who enslaved us!

▲ *Elijah Muhammad.*

Muhammad was a car worker who became leader of the Black Muslims. This was a militant group, started in the 1930s, which believed in **Black Separatism**.

Malcolm X joined the Black Muslims while in prison for burglary. When he split with Elijah Muhammad and tried to form a new group, he was murdered by Black Muslims.

> We do not want to mix with Whites and don't want them telling us what we can and can't do. We will use violence to defend ourselves against them if we have to!

▲ *Malcolm X.*

> I want to see Black Power! Black Power! Don't be pushed around by Whites! Use violence if you have to and take over the areas you live in!

▲ *Stokely Carmichael.*

Stokely Carmichael had been a student at an all-Black university. He became president of the SNCC and pushed every White member out of that organisation.

H. Rap Brown followed Stokely Carmichael as president of the SNCC.

We are sick of what we suffered at the hands of Whites. Arm yourselves – and kill the honkies! [White people]

▲ H. Rap Brown.

▲ Bobby Seale (left) and Huey Newton (right).

What good is non-violence? The police use violence against Black people all of the time. We are going to stop this. We'll fight back! We demand land, housing, education and justice!

Newton and Seale founded the Black Panther Movement in 1966.

One day I hope that Black and White people can live together in peace.

Martin Luther King did not agree with any of these people. As we have seen in an earlier chapter, he believed that all protests should follow Christian beliefs and be non-violent. He hoped to heal the hurt between Black and White people.

If Whites attack you – do not lower yourself by hitting back. If you keep calm, the world will admire this – and those who have hurt you will be seen as thugs.

▲ Martin Luther King.

**Q**

**1.** Write a script for a television debate between Martin Luther King and any two of the militant leaders featured in this section. You need to explain:

■ The arguments King would have used in favour of non-violence;

■ What each of the militants would have said to King and how he might have replied.

NOTE: you may need to refresh your memory of events in Chapters 4 and 5.

**2.** Using role play, present your debate in class.

# *Black Americans today ...*

INVESTIGATION

## EVIDENCE 1

In 1991 four White Californian policemen were videoed beating a Black man called **Rodney King**. At their trial, they were found 'not guilty' by a jury containing ten White people. After the verdict, many Black people in Los Angeles rioted. A new trial was held and this time two of the police were found guilty.

## EVIDENCE 4

In 1994 American Football star **O.J. Simpson**, was arrested for the murder of his wife and her male friend. Despite a lot of evidence against him, Simpson was acquitted by a jury containing nine Black people. A White detective had found important evidence against Simpson, but it was shown he held anti-Black views.

## EVIDENCE 2

In 1998 three White men linked to the Ku Klux Klan chained **James Byrd**, a disabled Black man, to the back of their truck and dragged him along a country road until he died.

## EVIDENCE 3

In February 2000, four New York policemen were found innocent of the murder of **Ahmed Amadou Diallo**, a Black suspect. Diallo was shot 19 times. Appeals for calm were made and there were no riots.

### EVIDENCE 5

White men:  3.5%
Black men:  7.9%
White women: 3.1%
Black women: 6.9%
White teenagers: 13.2%
Black teenagers: 25.0%

▲ *Unemployment in the USA, February 2000. Information from the NAACP.*

### EVIDENCE 6

1967  Thurgood Marshall becomes a Supreme Court Judge.
1969  James Clark Evers becomes Mayor of Fayette, Mississippi.
1977  Andrew Young becomes US Ambassador to the UN.
1989  Douglas Wilder becomes Governor of Virginia. Colin Powell becomes top US army commander. David Dinkins becomes Mayor of New York.
1992  Carole Moseley Braun becomes first Black woman senator.
1993  Toni Morrison wins Nobel Prize for Literature.

### EVIDENCE 7

*General Colin Powell* became a US army general in 1989 and Chairman of the Joint Chiefs of Staff in 1989.

### EVIDENCE 8

*Michael Johnson*, brilliant Black US athelete, became the first person ever to win a gold medal for both the 200m and 400m at the 1996 Olympics.

### EVIDENCE 9

*Toni Morrison's* novels explore what it is like as a Black person to face racism.

## INVESTIGATION

**You are the investigator!**

**1.** Split your class in half. One half investigate the events on this page and elswhere in Chapter 6 to make the case that 'Black people have overcome the forces that tried to hold them down'. The other half make the case that 'Black people have still got many obstacles to overcome'.

**2.** Then write your own report: *How much has changed for Black Americans since the end of slavery?*

■ Describe the situation then.
■ Explain attempts to overcome these problems.
■ Describe areas of life that have changed.
■ Describe problems yet to be overcome.
■ Decide *how much* life has improved.

# Index

# Kawaii
# NEEDLE
# FELTING

Felt 20 good luck charms
from around the world

HÉLÉNA ZAÏCHIK

DAVID & CHARLES
—PUBLISHING—

www.davidandcharles.com

# CONTENTS

# INTRODUCTION

Dear Reader,

You can't begin to imagine how happy it makes me to be writing these lines, the culmination of a love affair with a material and a technique whose origins are lost in history. I discovered them quite by chance a few years ago and they have profoundly transformed my creativity. However, it is also the fruit of a great deal of perseverance in terms of sharing my enthusiasm and passing on my deep conviction that wool – in carded form – is, and must be, one of the materials of the future in creative hobby crafts.

In the step-by-step projects and tips that follow, I hope to help you discover just how much this soft, comforting material can be used to bring the fruits of imagination to life, as long as you understand the mechanical process of felting and grasp the limited range of techniques required to master it.

I chose the theme of good-luck charms and talismans because I know that people often want to make a small gift for someone they love, but lack the time or budget to embark on something more complicated. It is a universal subject that takes you across the world, and says so much about our humanity and its thirst for happiness, even in these troubled times.

This book contains some quick and easy projects, suitable even for absolute beginners. However, there are also some more elaborate options, because if there is one thing I know for sure, it is that very soon, just like me, you won't be able to put your felting needles down again!

Several artists and creators that I admire have kindly offered me one of their lucky-charm or talisman designs to bring to life in 3D. I am infinitely grateful to them. Who could resist anything so cute?

I hope you enjoy making these talismans as much as I have enjoyed creating them for you.

Now, needles at the ready!

# WHY WOOL?

**I am going to tell you why I love carded wool so much and why you too will fall head over heels for this ecologically sound and sustainable material!**

## WHAT IS CARDED WOOL?

All the projects in this book involve a single main medium: carded wool. It is an eco-friendly material that has been around since the dawn of time.

Behind this mysterious name lies a material you all know but rarely see. Carded wool refers to wool at one of the very first stages in the manufacture of balls of spun yarn.

After the sheep have been sheared, the fleeces are sorted to remove any parts that are too dirty or damaged. The wool is then washed to remove all impurities and as much as possible of the lanolin, the grease that provides a natural protection for the animal's fleece and skin.

It is at this stage that the wool is passed through large, spiked rollers known as carders. The term comes from the Latin *carduus*, meaning thistle, a plant which was used in days gone by to comb out the wool. This process loosens the curls and spreads the wool over the entire surface of the rollers to form a soft, homogenous mat, which you can buy from suppliers in the form of a batt or roving folded into large balls for needle felting. The carded wool is also combed and spun into the knitting yarn that everyone is familiar with, of course.

Carded wool is a noble material and the fruit of the labour of careful breeders. There can be no such thing as good wool unless the animals are healthy and reared in conditions that meet their needs. The growing number of breeders who decide to add value to their herd's wool find they need to radically rethink their working methods, to ensure they reap the benefits of higher standards of animal welfare.

## A SIMPLE, DURABLE MATERIAL THAT REQUIRES NO MAINTENANCE

The soft, fragile appearance of wool belies its true nature: it is a robust and virtually invulnerable material.

It is antistatic so does not attract dust. It is also oil resistant, which makes it impervious to greasy stains. This means that anything you make will not require any maintenance and will effortlessly stand the test of time, despite its feather weight and delicate appearance.

## A NON-ALLERGENIC, POLLUTION-REMOVING MATERIAL

Did you know that the complex molecular structure of wool makes it depolluting, helping reduce the levels of formaldehyde and nitrogen dioxide in our homes?

Also, contrary to popular belief, wool is non-allergenic, as well as being antistatic and regulating humidity levels.

For all these reasons, I fell in love with wool and needle felting: a 100% manual and mechanical process that uses no chemicals or additives and no water.

# TESTIMONIALS

## WHAT ATTRACTED YOU TO NEEDLE FELTING?

### Camille instagram @1000et1etoiles

*I was inspired to give it a go after seeing some very pretty things made from carded wool, especially little animals. If you want to try it yourself, I would recommend starting on a smaller project that you love the look of, particularly in terms of colours. It is a stress-free creative hobby because mistakes can always be rectified.*

### Magali instagram @magalimaman

*I find needle felting a very easy technique to master, which can quickly give you some lovely results. You can make flat felt items (which I like to combine with embroidery) or ones in 3D. I'd recommend starting with tutorials – Héléna Zaïchik's videos show you how it is done. The most important thing is just to get started! Carded wool is a very forgiving material, which is great when you're learning a new technique. You can go back to something you are working on, add material, take it away, etc. I am very critical about what I make, but it must be said that I was amazed to see what I managed to achieve by following her advice.*

### Charlotte instagram @cha_labat

*I was inspired to try this technique by my love for all textile arts in general. A long time ago, someone very special to me gave me a boiled-wool necklace and I immediately loved the material. I find it warm. It is very easy and affordable for everyone, unlike dressmaking, for example, which requires much more equipment and technical mastery. I recommend choosing good quality tools and materials and taking a few classes to get a good feel for the material from the outset.*

### Géraldine instagram @la.princesse.au.pois.chiche

*Felted wool is a material that I think I love as much subjectively as objectively. I adore its misty, ethereal, dreamlike aspect... I find it very inspirational! You have to see it for yourself, and give it a try, to realise just how solid the things you can create from this ethereal material really are. Unlikely as it may seem, it is actually quite easy, and it reaps quick rewards!*

### Anne instagram @anneuneroseunefee

*I love handling this material, especially with its moisturising effect on my hands. I also really like the wide choice of colours (important in ensuring the realism of what I make). It doesn't cost much to get started and offers almost unlimited creative possibilities. Mistakes can always be rectified. Before you begin, find some attractive wool, a good teacher or good tutorial, and something simple but beautiful that you want to make, because it takes time. Don't get discouraged, take the time to look at your work with fresh eyes to see how improvements can be made. There is often a moment when you think it's not going to work, and then suddenly it just clicks. The end result may sometimes be a little different from the model, but is always interesting.*

### Valentine instagram @happy_as_a_bee_

*It was the desire to make Christmas decorations that motivated me to start needle felting. It is an ultra-accessible, fun, creative hobby, so don't hesitate to get started!*

**Michelle Provençal** (interior decorator & designer) instagram @thirdlee_co

*I discovered needle felting by chance, while doing some research online. I soon realised how accessible it was, so I followed some tutorials and quickly grasped the basic techniques. I chose wool because it was an unfamiliar medium for me, and I wanted to learn to work with a new material and be able to build on my mistakes.*

**Winnie Chui** instagram @feltbywinnie

*I discovered needle felting during a trip to Finland, where I bought my first pieces. Then, while travelling in Japan, I fell under the spell of their little felt animals, and decided to learn how to do it for myself. My son, who lives in Japan, sent me books and materials; I'm self-taught. I work with wool because it is a natural material and has such a sculptural quality; there are no limits to colour or shape – anything is possible! And most importantly, if something goes wrong, you can always go back and redo it.*

**Nastasya Shulyak** instagram @stowaways_toys

*I spent my childhood in Lithuania, a country where handicrafts play an important role, but I had never tried felting. Then, 13 years ago, I received some carded wool as a New Year's present. I can't explain the feeling of love at first sight I experienced – but it proved to be an enduring passion!*

**Marta Corada** instagram @Mei ♡ Mei

*I discovered felted wool from photographs, then I saw the work of a wool artist and was fascinated by the material's sculptural possibilities and its texture. I work in wool, among other media, because it allows me to render the anatomical details that I've studied so much in drawing, and its matt texture gives incredible depth to the colours. A tactile quality is one that I very much seek in my work.*

# EQUIPMENT

**You need very little to start needle felting!**

Creative hobbies can soon start requiring a lot of equipment and become expensive, but this is not at all the case for needle felting with carded wool.

Apart from the wool, you will need very few tools, and those that you do need are easy to use. If, at the outset, you are a little unsure, and don't want to invest, I have given a few tips for using what you already have at home.

## 1 FELTING NEEDLES

The only essential purchase is felting needles. I recommend buying at least three to six to start with, as you may break a few at first while you are getting the hang of the technique.

Most suppliers offer three needle gauges: fine (size 42), medium (size 40) and large (size 38). If you are just starting out, I recommend you just buy the size 42s. They are thin but versatile, and for a long time these were the only ones I used. 42-gauge needles can do everything and are essential for working on the small details and decorations of your projects; what is more, they leave very few marks on the surface of your work. 40-gauge needles are used to make slightly larger shapes, and have the advantage over the 42-gauge of making the work a little faster. As for 38-gauge needles, I use them very little. They are useful for felting large pieces through to the core and good for use on thick fibres if you are working with rustic wools. However, this is rare when you are a beginner. If you have several different gauges of needle, help distinguish them by putting a small piece of masking tape or a dab of nail varnish at the top for each needle size.

## 2 FOAM BLOCKS

Foam blocks act as a mat and allow you to poke with your felting needles without the risk of them breaking. These foam pads, which have a density specially designed for this work, can be found in any hobby shop that sells carded wool. If you don't have access to this type of foam, a household brush turned upside down might do the trick initially, or a big clean sponge, or even an old, slightly felted, folded jumper! The trick is to be able to poke your needles into the wool without breaking them, and without the material of your mat becoming entangled with your wool. If you opt for a foam pad, you will need to change it regularly as they usually wear out quite fast. If you want to give them a longer life, you could try covering them with a small, thick fabric cover that you can sew yourself to the appropriate size. Always keep one side of the foam block solely for working with white wool.

### 3 LEATHER FINGER PROTECTORS

These are completely optional but recommended, especially when you are just starting out, to protect your skin and avoid pricking yourself with your needles – a hazard which is particularly frequent in the early days. I absolutely recommend their use if needle felting with children (but this should only be done under your careful supervision, with children at least seven or eight years of age). If you don't want to invest, a gardening glove for the left hand (for right-handed people, and vice versa for left-handed people) can do the trick.

### 4 FELTING HANDLES

Finally, I must tackle the question of whether or not to use handles when needle felting. Initially, you can absolutely work with a single needle that you hold in your hand. But if you want to work faster, you may want to use several needles at the same time. You could then bunch three of them together with a small elastic band at the top, or invest in a plastic felting pen (unfortunately, as far as I know, you can't get a wooden version yet).

So I don't get the different needle sizes muddled up, and because I do a lot of felting and often travel with my work, I have purchased some wooden travel handles in which you can also store the needle for protection. I've even engraved the gauge onto the handles to remind me which needle I am using them for.

Finally, the much larger handles set with four to 20 needles (watch your fingers!) are best reserved for larger-scale projects that are not covered in this book.

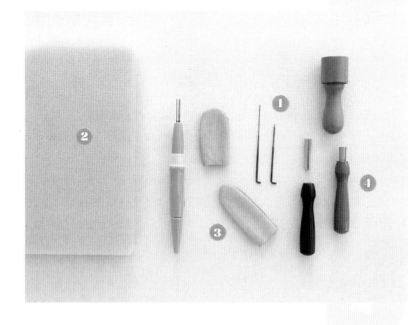

# CHOOSING YOUR WOOL

A LIVING MATERIAL: THERE IS NO SUCH THING AS SIMPLY 'WOOL', THERE ARE MANY DIFFERENT KINDS

Felted items are made using carded wool. As explained in Why Wool?, this is sheep's wool that has simply been washed, cleaned of its natural grease and impurities, and then combed. The appearance of the carded wool will vary depending on which part of the animal it comes from: the short hairs, close to the skin, give a soft, fine material, while the long hairs on its back are rougher and often thicker. So, you need to choose the specific type of wool to suit the project you want to work on. In its untreated form, wool will also vary according to the breed of sheep, the part of the fleece it comes from and the type of hair: white or brown, curly or straight.

## WHERE TO BUY YOUR WOOL

Don't worry, you don't need to have a sheep to hand! Carded wool is becoming increasingly available on crafting websites. There is no bad choice: all wools are easy to work with.

Some online suppliers of specialist wool can be found in Useful Addresses and Resources. Start with one or two balls, or a mini-assortment of several colours. All the wool used in this book comes from the Ô Merveille! shop in France, which is our partner in this work for materials. It offers Bergschaf wool from the Tyrol and Corriedale from New Zealand, and its wools are Oeko-Tex® certified. It supplies its wool in small batts folded into 30g balls, which is a practical format for beginners.

If you are lucky enough to have access to a farmer who can give you wool, check that the flock is in good health before you handle it, and opt to start with wool that has already been washed.

If you would like to find out more about sheep farming; whether or not to choose local breeds; determine your personal preferences (merino, Bergschaf, Shetland or other); learn how to understand labels and appellations; and find out more about washing methods and traditional wool dyeing, I recommend heading to my blog at: www.zaichik-diy.com.

## WHICH WOOL TO CHOOSE FOR EACH PROJECT

Felt artists generally prefer carded merino wool taken from the downy fleece of the animal's back. Wool from the outer coat is often interesting to use in its untreated, natural form to create particular effects, particularly in needle felting. For example, if it is curly, it can be used to imitate a poodle's coat or, if it is dark and coarse, it can be used to create the spines of a hedgehog.

## NATURAL AND PLANT DYES

Natural dyes have been around for centuries, particularly in France, where they were used to make the Gobelins and Aubusson tapestries. Mastering these dyeing techniques requires very specific raw materials and know-how. These dyed wools come at a cost that is out of the reach for most home crafters. Local wools that you can dye at home can be worth looking at; just bear in mind that they often fade quickly on exposure to light.

# TECHNIQUES

**1** HOW DEEP TO FELT

The principle of needle felting is to tangle the fibres of the wool together by catching them in the tiny harpoon-shaped notches along the shaft of your felting needle. The deeper you poke, the more you felt the core of your shape, thus creating a solid base. The more you stick to poking the surface, the more you felt the epidermis of what you are making, creating a kind of rigid skin over a soft core. You need to adapt how deeply you poke your needle to the area you wish to felt. We usually start by felting the core of a piece, then the surface.

Not felted enough

Not felted enough in the centre

Not evenly felted

Properly felted

**2** FLAT FELTING

It is generally a good idea to familiarise yourself with the use of felting needles by opting for a flat felting project to start with. This involves flattening out the wool from the fuzzy starting batt or roving. If you can, try to choose a project where you can shape the wool inside a cookie cutter. This is an excellent exercise for beginners.

All appliqué work on textiles (on a jumper or bag, for example) involves the flat felting technique. The poking of the needle causes the wool to penetrate the underlying textile, creating a kind of patch that fuses with the backing material.

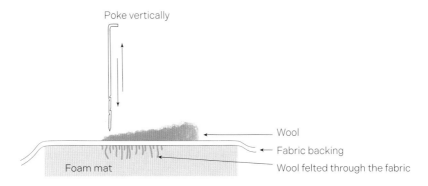

Poke vertically

Wool
← Fabric backing
Foam mat — Wool felted through the fabric

## ③ 3D FELTING

Making a 3D felted object is something of the Holy Grail! This enables you to make all the little figures and people, or miniature food items, that you often see on Pinterest, made by Slavic or Japanese crafters, for example. However this technique is no more complicated than flat felting and is sometimes even more fun, but you need a good understanding of the material and a familiarity with how it reacts to felting. Bear in mind that the wool becomes condensed in the area where you are felting, and therefore more relaxed on the opposite side, where you are not poking. This is the tension that you need to play with so you can gradually condense your wool and obtain the 3D shape you envisaged. As you felt, always keep a clear mental picture of the shape you are trying to achieve. As you progress, your hands will be guided by your mind quite naturally and you will no longer need to think about where to insert your needle. I always say that 3D felting is a little like moulding clay or playing with children's modelling dough. The most important thing, however, is to understand one essential movement: you must poke your needle in perpendicularly to the tangent of the curve you are seeking to obtain. If it has been a while since you studied geometry, here is a diagram to demonstrate this concept. If you remember just one thing – make it this!

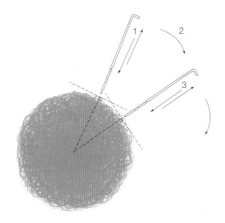

**4** MAKING A BALL

To get used to 3D felting, I would recommend starting with the ball exercise. It took me a long time to find the best technique for making a perfect ball just using a needle. I kept coming across unsightly folds of wool that appeared as I felted. Consequently, I would recommend my patented (lol) 'corolla' technique. This consists of taking a small batt of wool and folding it in on itself, while trying as much as possible to avoid wrinkles (photo 1). Then pinch the end in one hand (the aforementioned corolla) (photo 2). This means that you now have a ball to felt without it rolling around, and at the same time you can maintain a degree of tension so it holds its rounded shape. Then begin to poke all over the surface, perpendicularly to the tangent of the sphere, never stabbing more than once in the same place. Make a particular effort around the base of the corolla, as this is where the tension is greatest. If you use this method to felt the base of your ball really well, the rest will retain a beautiful, springy shape (photo 3). Now you simply need to trim your corolla a little (photo 4) then fold it against the surface of the ball and felt gently over it (photo 5). You can roll the finished ball between your fingers for a bit to make the shape completely uniform (photo 6).

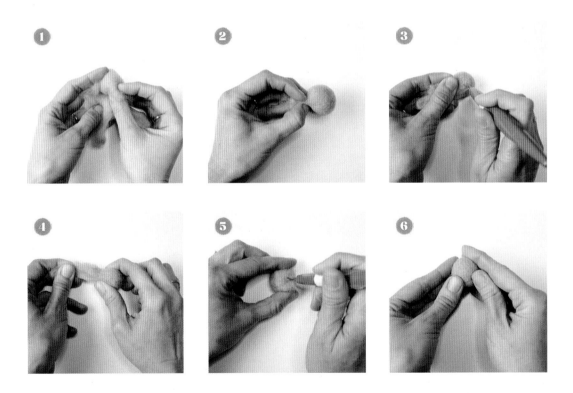

## ⑤ HOW TO ASSEMBLE THE HEAD AND BODY

You can also use the corolla technique (see Technique 4) to create solid joins between two 3D shapes, particularly if what you are making is intended for a child, because then the different parts cannot be pulled apart. To connect a head firmly to a body, start by felting a ball-shaped head, but leave the corolla sticking out, without folding it (photo 1). You will then roll the wool that will form the body around this safely anchored corolla (photo 2). Then felt the body (photo 3). During the mechanical process, the corolla and the fibres of the body will intertwine and form a single piece. The head and the body will then be one. You can do the same for the limbs, so arms and legs cannot be pulled off.

Alternatively, for purely decorative projects, you can fan out the corolla, until it is almost flat, placing it over the body at the place where the arms or legs are to be attached, and felting over it with a felting pen until the fibres are nicely intertwined.

## ⑥ EARS, WINGS, LEAVES…
### PIECES WITH FINE EDGES

When I first discovered needle felting, I swooned at the birds some artists made, with each feather felted separately, and couldn't understand how it was possible to needle felt such fine things without cruelly stabbing my fingers! The solution to obtaining a fine edge (for example, if you are making a leaf, or a figure's ear) is to pinch the wool very tightly then felt into this thickness. To protect yourself as you do this, you can put on a thick pair of leather gloves or some leather finger protectors (photo 1), or trap your wool between two pieces of cardboard (photo 2) before felting.

### 7 FORMING THE DETAILS

In this book, you will find many of the projects require you to add fine, delicate details to the surface of your felted 3D shapes. If until now I have compared needle felting to modelling, I now need to change my terms of reference: I prefer to compare the surface decoration to painting or even drawing, when I am creating very fine details such as little lines, or eyes, for example. First of all, bear in mind that you can only apply decorative details if your base is firm enough to ensure that the details don't simply sink into the main body when you felt. I remember working the seeds of a halved fig one by one and they all disappeared into the thick body of my fruit! Once your 3D shape is firm, but not too firm (sorry, nothing is simple at this stage!), because the detail would not attach well to an over-felted surface, apply the wool in tiny amounts (sometimes just a few fibres). Poke deeply initially, to secure the ends of your decorative details (photos 1 and 2) then continue felting with gentle little superficial pokes, round the outside of the shape or feature (photo 3), as if you were drawing a dotted line along the edges. If you want to refelt an item that has already been decorated, to make it smaller for example, be extremely careful when you are going over decorative details so your handiwork is not destroyed. If this stage gives you cold sweats initially, you can always simply embroider the details with an embroidery needle!

# MY TOP 10 TIPS
## ADVICE AND GOOD PRACTICE FOR PROGRESSING

### TIP 1
### Mixing colours

Do not hesitate to mix colours to create more shades. You can invest in a pair of small carding combs to mix different shades of wool and make your own colours. Playing with transparencies is another way to enrich your palette.

### TIP 2
### Store light and dark colours separately

Always keep the light colours separate from the dark when you are storing or working with your wools. Make sure you always have a foam mat that you use exclusively for white wool and nothing else. This will prevent your immaculate creation from being marred by tiny, coloured fibres.

## TIP 3
# Attaching a detail

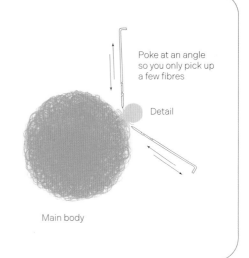

Poke at an angle so you only pick up a few fibres

Detail

Main body

If you want to attach a tiny 3D detail to an object that you have already felted, such as a little ball for a nose, poke into the base of your ball at an angle, so you only pick up a few fibres at a time, and turn it as you go. This will ensure you don't flatten the ball as you attach it and it will stay nice and round. Take note, however, this technique will not work for objects that will be handled a great deal, as the detail may loosen over time.

## TIP 4
# Spiral technique

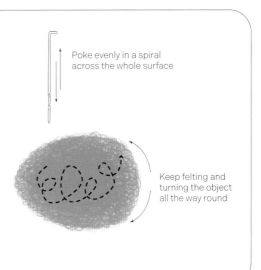

Poke evenly in a spiral across the whole surface

Keep felting and turning the object all the way round

To ensure a perfectly finished surface on a shape you have felted, I recommend using my 'spiral' technique: poke your needle in and out extremely superficially across the whole surface, moving it randomly in a series of small spirals. If it is a 3D shape, remember to tilt your needle at the appropriate angle (see Technique 3) as you are working these spirals, so you don't flatten out or change the shape.

## TIP 5
# Creating a narrowing

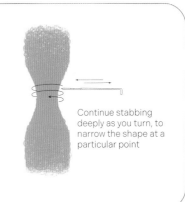

Continue stabbing deeply as you turn, to narrow the shape at a particular point

If you want to create a 'neck' in a 3D shape such as a ball or an egg, make deep pokes with your needle along a circular line as you turn the shape. Work right round your shape several times. The indent will get gradually deeper and narrower.

## TIP 6
# Making a 3D shape with edges

ℓℓ

I found it difficult to make cubes or pyramids or other geometric shapes with edges at first. To achieve this, simply apply the principle of poking in the needle perpendicularly to the plane of the surface you want to create. So to make a cube, you need to poke at 90° to each face from a starting ball. Little by little, the planes of the sides of your cube will start appearing. Only at the end can you pinch the edges a little so you can poke gently inside and stabilise them with delicate felting. I grant that it is clearly not the easiest felting exercise if you do not have a frame underneath, but you will get there with a little patience.

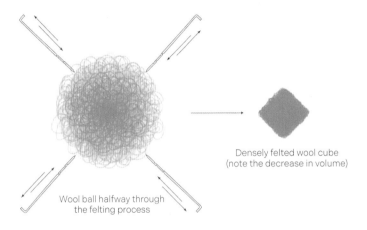

Densely felted wool cube
(note the decrease in volume)

Wool ball halfway through
the felting process

## TIP 7
# Avoid taking too much wool

ℓℓ

A strange rule, but one that is confirmed each time I do needle felting... When you want to create a detail, take a pinch of wool, then divide it in two. Generally this will give you just the right amount to make your detail.

## TIP 8
## Kneading wool

Often, when I want to make a more complicated shape, I knead my wool (just as if I am working with clay) to get the fibres going in the required direction. It is a bit like getting the material to understand what you want – you then just need to felt it into this position to ensure it holds its shape.

## TIP 9
## Save time

Felting involves driving out the air that sits between the fibres, by making them clump together. The more you form a tightly wound mass of wool before you start working with your needle, the faster the felting process will be.

## TIP 10
## Steam iron your projects

Don't hesitate to press your projects, with an iron set to maximum steam. This works particularly well on 2D items such as appliqué on a piece of clothing or a bag. I am often asked whether you can iron wool, and the answer is that nothing could be better than a bit of steam, precisely because you want it to felt. Indeed, don't hesitate to iron your projects, pressing firmly to create a nice, neat surface finish.

# FAQ

### How should I clean my needle-felted objects?

A hand-felted piece shouldn't really get dirty, but if you want to wash your item anyway, I recommend using a soft cloth and gently rubbing the surface. Your wool is already felted but if it is not very firm, the small details might move. Do not even consider putting felted objects through the washing machine. Some crafters like to felt with a needle then felt further using soap and water to make it even more solid. This results in a very hard, hairy piece, which I personally am not that keen on, but it can certainly be done.

### Hard or soft, when should I stop felting?

There is no answer to this question. Some people like very hard creations where the wool is tightly condensed, while others prefer softer, more springy shapes. As time goes by, you will find your own style and decide whether you prefer softer, fuzzier sculptures or harder, smoother pieces. You must also remember that a very dense object will need much more wool for a single project than a soft one. The wool weights given are therefore by way of indication only; everything depends on your personal felting style. One thing to remember, however, is that if you want to add details to a piece, you need to add them before it gets too hard and felted, so the new elements adhere well to the base. Once the details have been added, if you want a very firm end result, you need to continue felting the entire surface, but proceed delicately so as not to destroy the details as you felt them. With time, you will find the right techniques; in the meantime, when you are starting out, you can embroider or sew any details that seem too fine and difficult to add to what you are making.

### What quantity of wool is required?

This is a question that comes up time and again, and is closely linked to the previous one. Consider that when you are felting, you are expelling the air that is in your batt of wool. In order to find out roughly what volume of wool you will end up with after felting, squeeze your wool sample in your fist: the volume contained within your hand is the one that you will achieve with the quantity of wool you have selected.

### Should I shave my finished project?

When I first discovered carded wool, I could not understand how the artists that I admired managed to obtain such smooth sculptures without the fuzz that stood out all over mine. Sadly, I found there is no secret to share: for a very smooth sculpture, you need to carry on felting until nearly all the tiny fibres of wool are worked in and felted! By contrast, shaving what you have made, or trimming with an anti-pilling device, often gives a disappointing result in my opinion, because all the fibres are cut to the same length and end up being more obvious than they were before.

Shaving does not make a surface that has been insufficiently felted more attractive. Some makers might add glue to their sculpture to get rid of the fuzz, but I am not keen on this process as it involves adding a polluting and chemical element to a natural, noble material.

### Why is my shape sagging?

If you are working on a 3D shape but it has a tendency to sag and collapse, this is simply because you are not holding your needle perpendicular to the tangent of the curve that you are trying to form (see Technique 3). If you always poke in the same direction, the wool condenses, forming a flat area that becomes hollow instead of staying nicely rounded. Remember to move your needle around the surface, changing the angle at which you poke with your needle.

### How can I protect my lucky charms from moths?

Just like woollen jumpers, items made from carded wool must be protected from moths. If you want to avoid buying chemical repellents, I recommend adding a few drops of cedar essential oil to the back of what you have made every three months or so. Note that moths hide in dark, confined places, so storing your lucky charms somewhere light should be sufficient to ward them off, and they are much less likely to suffer moth damage than if they are left in the bottom of a drawer. Of course, if you take your lucky charms everywhere with you, they will be as safe as can be!

### Does it matter if my wool has some impurities?

I am often asked whether it is a problem having grass or little bits of plant matter in the wool that you buy. In my experience, this sort of debris tends to come to the surface as you carry out the felting process, as the bits are not susceptible to felting. So, on the whole I would say no. Moreover, the more carefully sorted the wool, the more expensive it is, as sorting is always done by hand. I just have one caveat, for light or pastel colours, especially white: if using these shades, try to opt for wool that has been well sorted because your needles can break up these small bits, which then get inextricably tangled in the fibres, leading to what look like stains on the light wool.

### How can I remove needle marks?

I am often asked how to remove needle marks, and I asked myself the same question when I first started. In reality, it isn't much of a problem – you simply need to give the surface of your work a little rub with your fingertips and the marks will fade. This might not be so easy if you are working with big needles, but as you normally only use these on the base of large-scale pieces, the marks are covered with finer wool afterwards.

# PROJECTS

# SAKURA

*The cherry blossom (sakura) season, which the Japanese celebrate as hanami, is a period in springtime when you feel reborn, and everything seems possible again. I have always loved the fragility of these fleeting flowers, which remind us of the precious and ephemeral nature of beauty.*

**Difficulty level :**
A beginner's project that combines embroidery, beads and felted wool, and provides an introduction to mixing colours.

## Wool

• 2g of pale pink wool
• 2g of natural white wool

## Equipment

• One medium 40-gauge needle
• Felting pen fitted with three 40-gauge needles
• A few seed beads in shades of pink
• Gold or copper-coloured metallic embroidery thread
• Beading needle
• Embroidery needle
• Matching sewing thread
• Foam mat
• Brooch back

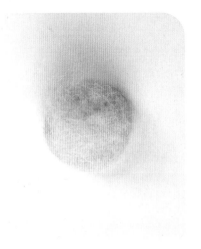

**1 •** Form the pale pink wool into a large ball and felt it gently so it becomes fairly firm, with a nice, neat surface. Refer to Techniques 3 and 6 to remind yourself how to angle your needle and create attractive edges.

**2 •** Place a small pinch of natural white wool in the centre of your ball and felt into place. Use the felting pen to ensure an even finish.

**3 •** Using a single needle, poke defined lines to form your ball into five petals, as shown in the photo. Keep going until your pattern is very clear.

**4 •** Embroider with the metallic thread, passing a thread along each groove. Bring the thread back out through the centre, forming several loose loops that you will then cut to make the stamens.

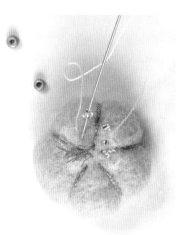

**5** • To accentuate the resemblance to real cherry blossoms, I also used matching thread to sew on a few seed beads around the centre of the flower. Decorate according to your taste and the materials you have to hand.

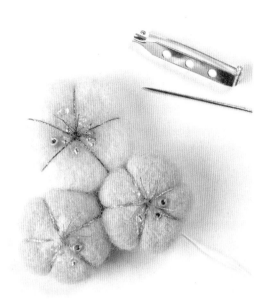

**6** • Make two more flowers in different sizes or colours, then sew them all together. Finally, simply sew on to a brooch back to complete your lucky-charm *sakura* brooch.

# GANESH

*The elephant is a symbol of strength, constancy and prosperity in many Asian countries and religions, and is omnipresent in their decorations and artwork. I have imagined one just for you – he is a chubby, smiley fellow, to give confidence to the lucky recipient.*

**Difficulty level :**
A project to practise making little *kawaii* animals.

## Wool

• 9g of sand-coloured wool
• Small handful of bright yellow wool
• Small handful of apricot-coloured wool
• Small handful of pink wool
• Small handful of pumpkin-coloured wool
• Pinch of pale pink wool
• Pinch of dark grey wool

## Equipment

• One medium 40-gauge needle and/or one fine 42-gauge needle
• Felting pen fitted with three 40-gauge needles
• Foam mat

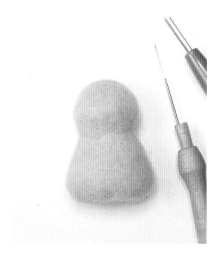

**1 •** Divide your sand-coloured wool in two. Take one half and form a slightly flattened pear shape, as shown in the photo, using Technique 4. This will be the head.

**2 •** Divide your remaining wool in two again. Take half and roll it around the corolla of the head, to form the elephant's body (see Technique 5).

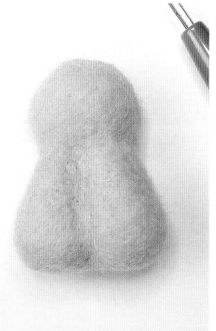

**3 •** On one side of the elephant's body, felt the spine and the buttocks by making a vertical indent down the middle of the body.

**4** • Next, divide the remaining sand-coloured wool into five roughly equal parts. Setting aside one part for making the elephant's trunk, cheeks and ears, use the other four parts to make the legs. Fold each in two horizontally, then roll it up to obtain a cylindrical leg, flattened at one end.

**5** • Repeat four times to make the front and back legs. Felt, turning them as you move round with your felting pen, so they end up fairly slender and nicely cylindrical.

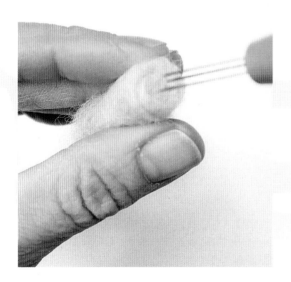

**7** • Now firmly attach each leg in an arc around the elephant's body. Stab hard into the edges until the legs are securely fixed to the body.

**6** • For the soles of the feet, felt the end of each leg flat with the felting pen.

**8** • Roll the trunk in the same way as the legs, but shorter and narrower, then attach it to the front of the head. Shape the end into a nice curve as shown in the photo.

**9** • Referring to Technique 2, felt each ear flat separately on a foam mat. Make sure that they are symmetrical by using an equal amount of wool for each one. Leave a corolla at the base of each ear.

**10** • Fan out the corolla, and felt through it to attach the ears to the head.

**11** • Now you can create a defined line around your elephant's wrists and ankles by stabbing firmly round each limb, approximately 5mm (¼in) from the ends, so that a slight indent in the wool is formed round them. If needed, add a tiny bit of wool to the cheeks to make them chubbier.

**12 •** Flat felt four small rounds of decreasing circumference in the four colours of wool shown in the photo. The diameter of the biggest round should be roughly equivalent to the space between your elephant's ears.

**13 •** Stack the four rounds on top of each other and attach them to the elephant's head by poking your needle through the edges of each circle at an angle.

**14 •** Now, using the point of your needle, you can pull out a few strands of wool from each round so they are pointing downwards towards the elephant's trunk. Then add a tiny ball in a contrasting colour to each level of the crown. Follow Tip 3 to attach them (see My Top 10 Tips).

**15 •** Make a few more little balls in the bright yellow wool and attach them to one of your elephant's wrists.

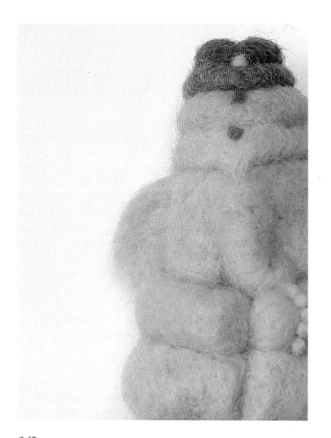

**16 •** Add a tiny bit of pale pink to the inside of each of the elephant's ears.

**17 •** Roll some tiny pieces of dark grey wool between your fingers to form the eyes. Attach them to the elephant's face along with a little dot in the middle of his forehead. Give him a funny expression by trying out a few shapes and positions for the eyes.

## 360° views

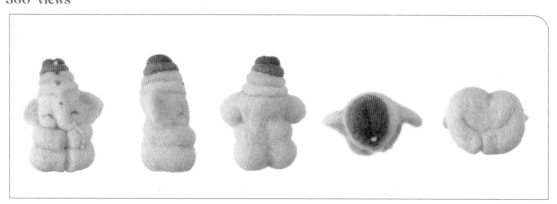

# FOUR-LEAF CLOVER

A rare mutation of the common clover or the shamrock, the four-leaf clover is considered lucky in many places, and in Ireland, where the shamrock is the national emblem, it is strongly associated with St Patrick's Day. It should not be confused with oxalis, often sold as a 'shamrock plant', but which is in fact unrelated.

**Difficulty level :** ●
A beginner's project to help you get to grips with flat felting using a mould. This technique allows you to achieve a complex shape quite easily.

## Wool

• 1g of leaf green wool and a pinch of moss green
• 1g of moss green wool and a pinch of leaf green

## Equipment

• One medium 40-gauge needle and one fine 42-gauge needle
• Felting pen fitted with three 40-gauge needles
• Shamrock-shaped biscuit-cutter (available from culinary equipment sites)
• Foam mat
• Two blank barrette hair clips of your choice
• Glue gun

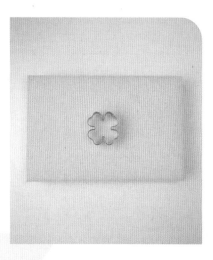

**1 •** Place your shamrock-shaped cookie cutter on the foam mat.

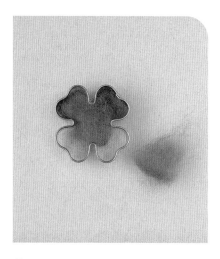

**2 •** Fill it with green wool, pinch by pinch, as shown in the photo, until it is approximately two thirds full.

**3 •** Felt vertically using the felting pen, taking care not to catch the metal with your needles, which might cause them to break.

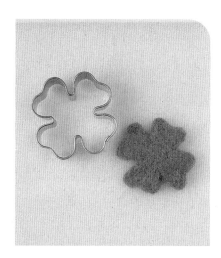

**4 •** Remove the cookie cutter, flip your shape over and pop it back inside the cutter, so you can felt both sides and prevent the wool from becoming too entangled with the foam.

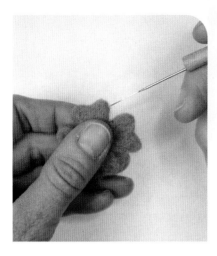

**5** • Tuck in any wool that sticks out beyond the edges, pinching your clover leaf and felting with a fine needle. Watch out for your fingers! You can use Technique 6.

**6** • Separately, felt four little teardrop shapes in the same green, and felt them onto your clover leaves, as shown in the photo, to give it some volume: one teardrop on one half of each leaf.

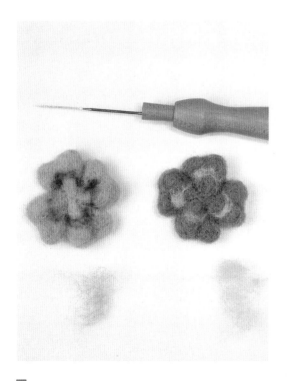

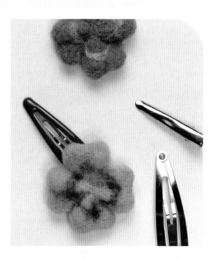

**8** • Using a glue gun, stick each shamrock to a blank barette hair clip.

**7** • Add and felt a tiny detail in your contrasting green wool. Use barely a wisp of wool. The photo gives you some idea of quantities. Make a second four-leaf clover in the same way, but reversing the colours.

# HAND OF FATIMA

*The Hand of Fatima is a symbol of protection for women and children often worn around the neck, particularly in North African countries. It frequently has an eye in its centre. Worn by followers of a number of religions, it has a significance and complex origins that are difficult to trace, but I have always loved this eminently feminine sign.*

**Difficulty level :** ●
A beginner's project to try out flat felting without a mould, start adding details and learn to work neatly in very contrasting wools.

## Wool

• 4g of black or very dark-coloured wool
• 1g of white or light-coloured wool

## Equipment

• One medium 40-gauge needle and one fine 42-gauge needle
• Felting pen fitted with three 40-gauge needles
• Foam mat (one reserved for dark colours, so you don't mark your work with any residual light-coloured fibres)
• Punch needle or knitting needle (to make a hole)
• Cord

**1** • Take half of your black wool, then divide this half into three equal parts.

**2** • Form each of these thirds into a long sausage. To do so, arrange each section of wool into a longish rectangle, and place it flat, facing you. Fold the top edge inwards, then roll the rectangle up. This will give you a sausage shape with a corolla at the bottom and a neat end at the top.

**3** • With the felting pen, felt these three sausage shapes, stabbing hard, to form the fingers. Follow Tip 5 to obtain narrow cylinders (see My Top 10 Tips), and don't hesitate to roll the sausages between the palms of your hands to help the wool compact before continuing the felting process with more pokes of the needle.

**4** • Now form the hand. Shape the remaining half of the black wool into a big square and then fold it in half. Position the three sausage fingers in the centre of the mass of wool that you have just folded, as shown in the photo. This will ensure that as you felt, the fibres will mix and the fingers will become solidly attached to the palm of the hand.

**5** • Continue felting, following the photo, to form the outline of the palm, the thumb and the little finger. To form the typical curves of this lucky charm, adjust the angle of your felting pen. Make sure you continue turning your shape so you work both sides. The felting should be firm enough to prevent the decorative designs added in steps 7 and 8 from sinking into the main body.

**7** • Now add the filigree decorations using Technique 7. Be patient, it takes a while to get the hang of this technique. Start by taking a few fibres of white wool to depict an eye in the middle of the palm. Use your finest needle (42-gauge). First make the outline of the eye, then a circle in the middle, as shown in the photo.

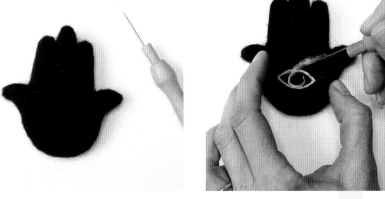

**Tip**
If you are more comfortable with embroidery, you can embroider the white motif rather than doing it in carded wool.

**6** • The fingertips are formed by felting patiently for some time with a single needle, while continuing to turn your work in your hands. Work around the tip of the thumb and the tip of the little finger to give them a nice symmetrical curve and a slight point.

**Note**
Adding a light colour on top of a dark one is one of the trickiest things to do, as the fibres must not mix. Once you have successfully completed this lucky charm, you'll have refined your skills to add appliqué decorations to what you make!

**8** • Add your own choice of further decorative touches. For example, I have added two bands round the end of the fingers and dots around the eye and down the back of the fingers, as shown in the final photo.

**9** • Finally, work a hole through the base of the hand with a punch needle or large knitting needle, then thread a cord through the hole and knot to the desired length.

# EVIL EYE

*These blue eyes, the Greek* matakia, *often made of glass, are symbols hung in houses or worn as jewellery to ward off bad influences or the evil eye. This symbol is widespread in Mediterranean areas and also evokes the eye colour of newborn babies and represents youth. An attractive gift for anyone you wish to protect.*

**Difficulty level :** ⬤
An easy project for a stress-free introduction to needle felting.

## Wool

• 3g of ultramarine blue wool
• Small batt of turquoise wool
• Small batt of white wool
• Pinch of black wool

## Equipment

• One medium 40-gauge needle
• Felting pen fitted with three 40-gauge needles
• Foam mat
• Punch needle or knitting needle (to make a hole)
• Leather cord

**1 •** This project uses the flat felting technique (see Technique 2). Start felting a batt of ultramarine blue wool on your foam mat.

**2 •** Fold the edges of the batt to the back to create an egg shape. Felt on both sides, turning your shape regularly to prevent the fibres from getting worked into the foam mat.

**3 •** Using the felting pen, and taking precautions to ensure you do not prick yourself (see Technique 6), now felt the edges of your shape to get a nice smooth finish, with no protruding fibres.

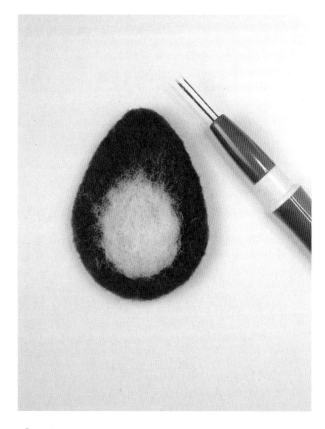

**4 •** Felt a small batt of white wool in the centre of the blue shape, as shown in the photo.

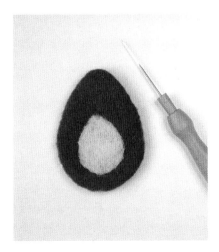

**5** • Using the single needle, go back over the edge of the white batt, poking at regular intervals to obtain a well-shaped oval.

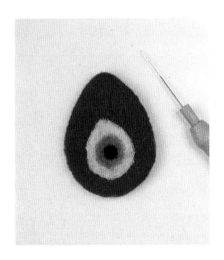

**6** • Repeat steps 4 and 5 with the turquoise blue wool to make the rounded shape of the iris, then add a dot of black wool for the pupil.

**7** • Finally, work a hole through the top of the shape by gently inserting and twisting a punch needle or large knitting needle, then thread the cord through the hole and knot to the desired length.

## Pattern for design detail

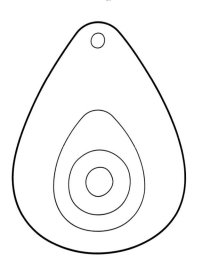

# MANEKI-NEKO

*The origin of this little Japanese cat, which is believed to bring luck and prosperity, seems to lie in numerous proverbs and legends. The colours and positions of its paws all have different significances; it is up to you to decide how you want them. Personally, I opted for the ones I found the most endearing!*

**Difficulty level :**
Very detailed step-by-step instructions make this the ideal project for creating your first *amigurumi* in carded wool.

## Wool

• 8g of white wool
• 1g of red wool
• 1g of coral-coloured wool
• 1g of caramel-coloured wool
• 1g of black wool
• 1g of yellow wool

You will not use up all the coloured wool; to estimate quantities, refer to the photos, which will give you an idea of the amount you need.

## Equipment

• One medium 40-gauge needle and one fine 42-gauge needle
• Felting pen fitted with three 40-gauge needles
• Embroidery needle and black embroidery thread

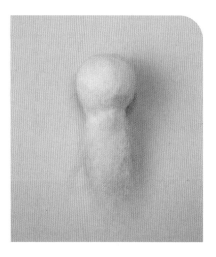

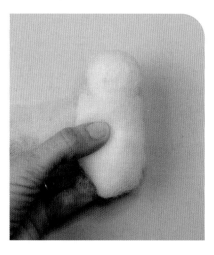

**1** • Take approximately one third of your white wool. Using Technique 4, form your cat's head, leaving the corolla sticking out.

**2** • Take a little over half the remaining white wool to make a body that is slightly bigger than the head. To attach the body and head, use Technique 5, wrapping the wool around the corolla.

**3** • Felt this wool into the shape of a ball to give your cat a nice round body. Remember to angle your felting pen towards the centre of the ball formed by the body, to ensure it is spherical, particularly around the join.

**4** • Add a horizontal batt of wool to the bottom of the face to build up the cheeks and muzzle, and carefully attach using the felting pen without losing too much of the volume. From this point on, don't hesitate to add or remove bits of wool to shape your maneki-neko's face and cheeks. A millimetre here or there often makes the difference between a cute expression and a neutral one.

**Tip**
Another option consists of felting the balls of the head and body separately, then joining them by wrapping one of the balls with a fine wool batt which can be felted on to the second.

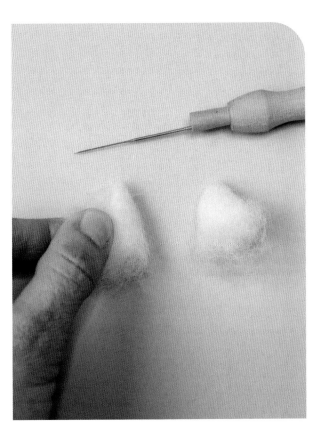

**6** • Attach the ears to the head ensuring they are symmetrical. To do so, fan out the wool corolla at the base of the ears, spread it against the top of the head and then felt gently through this batt to join it to the wool of the head without creating marked grooves along the join.

**5** • Fold two batts of white wool of approximately the same size into triangles, then felt the top of them hard to form pointed ears. Refer to Technique 6 for how to make felted pieces with fine edges.

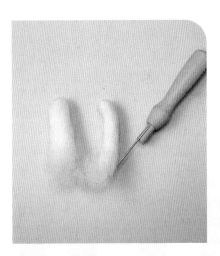

**7** • Form two elongated arms by rolling two small sausages of wool and rolling one of the ends of each in a little on itself to form the paws. Make the wrists by working your needle round just below the paw, using the 40-gauge needle (see My Top 10 Tips: Tip 5).

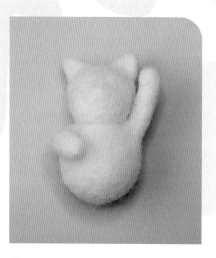

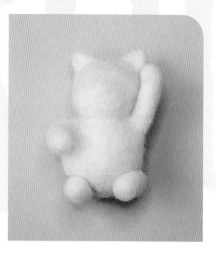

**8 •** Consider how you want to position the arms before attaching them using the corolla technique described in step 6. You do not need to attach them along their full length; just at the top of the arms is enough if you felt firmly.

**9 •** Shape and attach the legs in the same way as the arms, but this time, join them along the full length of the legs, so your cat keeps its balance once in position. Shaping the *maneki-neko* is complete – now you can decorate it.

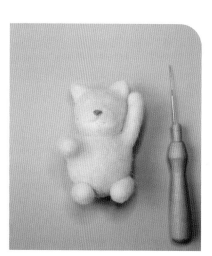

**10 •** Taking a little coral-coloured wool, make a small ball and attach it to the tip of the muzzle. (Refer to My Top 10 Tips: Tip 3 for how to attach small details to 3D shapes.) At this stage, you can mark the lines of the mouth by poking repeatedly along the outline you have designed.

**11 •** To highlight the mouth, felt a few fibres of red wool along the indented outline, using the fine (42-gauge) needle. I have shown how much wool I used in the photo so you can decide how much you need.

**12 •** For the eyes, make two tiny, elongated balls from the black wool and roll them between your fingers before attaching them gently using the 40-gauge needle. The eyes can be a little sunken. Refer to Technique 7 which explains how to add decorative details.

**13 •** Add some coral-coloured fibres to the inside of the ears and attach the pads to the raised front paw, using the same technique as for the eyes.

**14 •** Using a fine, long strip of red wool, attach the collar with a few pokes of the 40-gauge needle. Take particular care around the edges in order to obtain nice, clean lines and work in any protruding fibres.

**15 •** Decorate your cat as you please. I have chosen to give mine some caramel-coloured and black patches like the most traditional maneki-neko.

**16 •** Add the disc to the collar by forming a ball of yellow wool and flattening well before attaching.

**17** • Mark the grooves between the claws on each back leg using a thick needle if you have one, otherwise go over them several times to obtain neat indents.

**18** • Finally, using two strands of black embroidery thread, embroider whiskers on either side of your little cat's nose, as well as the lines marking the claws on the paws of its back legs. Conceal the knots of the thread within the bulk of the wool.

## 360° views

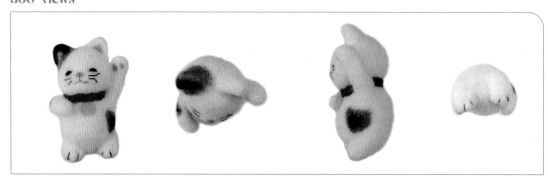

# SACRED HEART

The heart is a magical, mysterious organ that has fascinated humans since time immemorial. Whether or not it refers to the Sacred Heart of Jesus within the Christian tradition, I see this motif, a very common one in Eastern European folk art, as a universal symbol of love.

Creation by @ginacie
www.ginacie.blogspot.com

**Difficulty level :**
A project to help you progress your flat felting, and which confirms that you really can decorate anything with carded wool!

## Wool

- Small handful of red wool
- Pinch of bright green wool
- Pinch of turquoise wool
- Pinch of fuchsia-coloured wool
- Pinch of yellow wool

## Equipment

- One medium 40-gauge needle and one fine 42-gauge needle
- Felting pen fitted with three 40-gauge needles
- A felt hat
- Chalk marker (tailor's chalk) or heat-erasable pen
- A small foam ball or a small jumper
- Steam iron
- Embroidery needle and turquoise embroidery thread

**1 •** Transfer the design to the side of the crown of your hat. It is quite difficult to put a transfer on a hat, so start by simply drawing a large heart, then add the main details freehand. Place the small foam ball (or small jumper rolled into a ball) inside the hat to support it while you are felting.

**2 •** Place a fine, but not transparent, batt of red wool on the heart. Fold the edges of the heart inwards underneath the shape before starting to attach it around the edge, poking with the single 42-gauge needle at regular intervals. Then felt the whole surface so it penetrates the wool of the hat uniformly, using Technique 2.

**3 •** Add a narrow band of yellow wool round the outside of the red heart, poking repeatedly into the edges of each side to get a neat, flat finish.

**4 •** Now felt three pretty bright green leaves, this time forming the wool into ellipses with pointed ends.

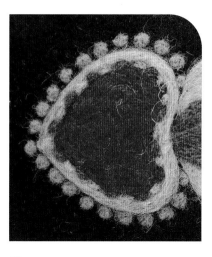

**5 •** Add three small stamens in fuchsia-coloured wool as shown in the photo.

**6 •** Decorate all round the outside of your heart with little balls of turquoise wool, rolled carefully between your fingers before you fix them in place with small pokes of the needle (see My Top 10 Tips: Tip 8). You need to take the time to poke around each ball to get a clean finish before felting the middle.

**7 •** Create a two-tone scalloped border along the inside edge of the yellow band, by making some tiny balls of wool and felting them on, one by one. I opted to alternate bright green and fuchsia. Then, add a yellow ball at the top of each pink stamen.

**8 •** You can now press your design with a steam iron to ensure it is nice and flat (see My Top 10 Tips: Tip 10). First check in an area that won't show that the iron/steam is not going to leave a mark on your hat. Finally, embroider the patterns on the heart, the stamen and the leaves. I have mainly used straight stitch, with daisy stitch leaves for the embroidery detail on the heart.

## Pattern for design detail

# LADYBIRD

*I remember from when I was a young girl the joy of one of these little ladybirds landing by chance on my finger. Whether or not this woollen ladybird will help your wishes come true, I hope that it will make you smile, even if it is not very effective against the aphids in your garden!*

## Wool

• 3g of red wool
• Small handful of black wool

## Equipment

• One medium 40-gauge needle and one fine 42-gauge needle
• Felting pen fitted with three 40-gauge needles
• Wire cutters and flat-nose pliers
• 13cm (5in) pliable metal wire in the colour of your choice

**Difficulty level :**
A very simple project teaching you how to felt over a metal frame.

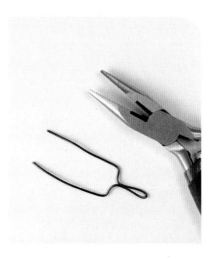

**1** • Fold the wire as shown in the photo, using flat-nose pliers to form neat angles.

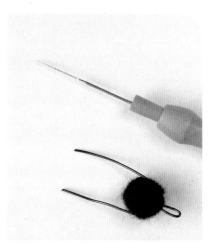

**2** • Roll a small batt of black wool tightly around your wire, as shown in the photo, leaving both ends of the wire protruding well beyond. The secret when working with a frame is to felt gently with a single needle, making sure you are poking accurately to avoid hitting the wire under the wool. Keep moving around the shape to ensure your ladybird's head is nice and round.

**3** • Now wrap the red wool tightly around at the base of the head, then felt it, taking the same precautions as in step 2. This time, try to make the top nice and rounded and the bottom flat, or even a little indented, for the ladybird's body.

**4** • Using the pliers, take the end of each length of wire and curve it backwards, rolling the end in on itself a little to form the antennae.

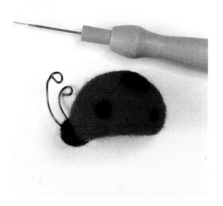

**5** • Now you simply need to add some little balls of black wool to make the ladybird's spots – you can vary the colours and shapes of the spots as you choose to. This ladybird can be worn as a brooch or on a hair clip, for example, or indeed, why not attach it to a hat?

## 360° views

# DOLPHIN

*Were you, like me, part of that generation of teenagers who had posters of dolphins on their bedroom walls? The Flipper Generation! Dolphins are good-luck animals in numerous cultures: symbols of virtue who remind us that we must protect our oceans at all costs.*

**Creation by @socroch**
www.socroch.fr

## Wool

• 7g of pale blue wool
• Small handful of white wool
• Pinch of pale pink wool
• Pinch of black wool

## Equipment

• One medium 40-gauge needle and one fine 42-gauge needle
• Felting pen fitted with three 40-gauge needles
• Keyring chain (optional)

**Difficulty level :**
A project to help you learn how to model simple shapes and connect them together.

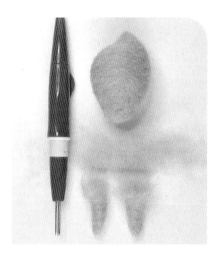

**1 •** Setting aside approximately one quarter of the pale blue wool, which you will use for the fins and the tail, use the rest to felt a lemon shape. To form this shape successfully, make sure the wool is tightly rolled from the start when you are making your basic ball (see My Top 10 Tips: Tip 9). Make one of the ends very pointed: this will be your dolphin's nose.

**2 •** Felt two small tail fins separately. To make them, roll the wool into a long, tight cone before you start felting. Leave a corolla at one end. You can then attach them to the body, wrapping a band of blue wool tightly around the corollas and the dolphin's tail end. Felt the join firmly.

**3 •** Felt another three fins separately: two side fins and one shorter, dorsal fin, which is broader at the base, as shown in the photo. Then fix them to the dolphin, fanning out the corollas over the body so the joins cannot be seen. The more symmetrical you can make it, the more attractive it will be.

**4 •** Place a fine layer of white wool under the dolphin's belly. Felt the edges securely using small pokes of a single needle to ensure a clean finish, then felt the whole surface with the felting pen.

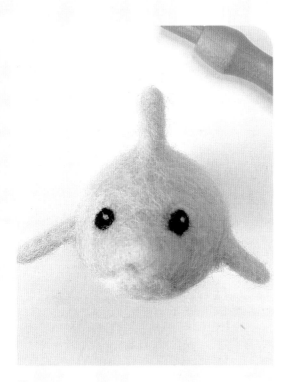

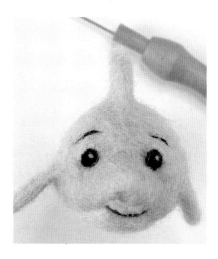

**6** • Felt pale pink cheeks under the eyes, as seen in the photo. Finally, add two fine wisps of black wool and felt them on with little pokes for the eyebrows and mouth.

**5** • For the eyes, felt two small discs of white wool then add two tiny black balls on top, referring to My Top 10 Tips: Tip 3 for how to attach them securely. Finish by adding a little glint in the eye by attaching a minuscule ball of white wool to each pupil. In this way, you get a finish that is similar to the safety eyes attached to crochet figurines, but made entirely of carded wool.

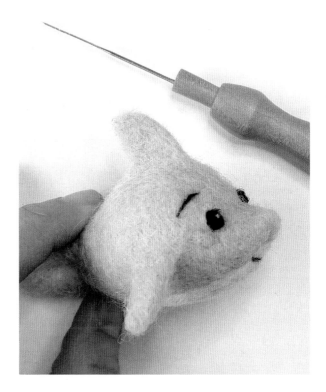

**Tip**
If you find it too tricky to add the facial details using wool, you can attach plastic or glass eyes and embroider the eyebrows and the mouth with black thread.

# DARUMA

These little figures, representing a Buddhist monk who meditated for so long that he lost the use of his arms and legs, are symbols of perseverance! Red is the colour of lucky charms in Asia, and they are meant to be placed within eyeshot to remind us that we need endurance to achieve our dreams and to try to achieve the goals that we have set ourselves.

## Wool

• 9g of white wool
• Fine batts of red wool
• Handful of black wool
• Handful of pale beige wool

## Equipment

• One medium 40-gauge needle and one fine 42-gauge needle
• Felting pen fitted with three 40-gauge needles

**Difficulty level :**
An interesting project for starting out in 3D felting.

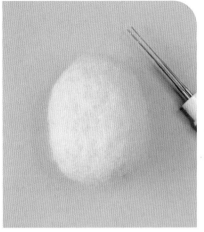

**1 •** Start by felting a big white egg. For this Daruma, you need the base shape to be solid. Refer to Technique 1 and the tip given here for adapting the felting pen to aid you.

**2 •** Using the single 40-gauge needle, mark out the Daruma's face on the egg, forming the grooves as shown in the photo. Mark the outlines of the face in the shape of a horizontal peanut, the eyes and nose as rounded bumps, and the underside of the nose like a horizontal curly bracket.

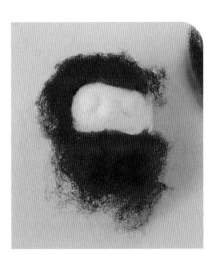

**3 •** To cover your Daruma's body in red, take some fine batts of wool and fold them in half. Place the straight edge of one of the folded batts against the outline of the face and felt along this edge. This is an easy way to get a neat outline.

**4 •** Cover the whole of your Daruma's body in red. Use fine, but not transparent, batts of wool and do not poke too hard, to ensure a nice smooth surface.

**5 •** To make the moustache and the eyebrows, roll a piece of black wool between your fingers before using a fine (42-gauge) needle to attach it in swoops, as shown in the photo. Try to make the shapes as symmetrical as possible. Refer to Technique 7.

**6** • Using pale beige wool, mark the outline of the eyes with a narrow border, then decorate your Daruma's body with small stripes on the stomach and either side of the face.

**7** • Place two little 'commas' of red wool at the base of the nose to highlight the nostrils.

**8** • Now it is time to make a wish and make the Daruma's first eye. Start by felting a black circle into the middle of the bump forming the eye, then two small dots of white, as in the photo, to put a glimmer in his eye... Now, wait until your wish comes true before completing the second eye!

## Pattern for design detail

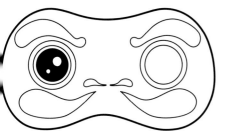

## 360° views

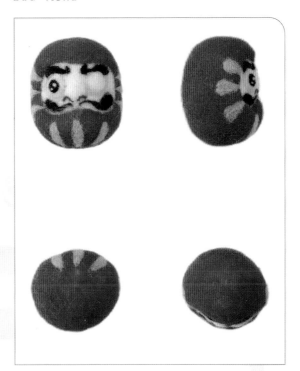

# DOVE OF PEACE

*I wanted a good-luck charm that represented peace... What could be more universally recognised as such than a gentle dove?*

**Creation by @ombeline_brun**
www.ombelinebrun.com

**Difficulty level :** ●●
The challenge of this project lies in taking time to master the complex flat-felted shapes and managing the proportions so the angles formed at the points of attachment remain faithful to the design.

## Wool
• 7g of white wool

## Equipment
• One medium 40-gauge needle and one fine 42-gauge needle
• Felting pen fitted with three 40-gauge needles
• Foam mat
• Gold metallic embroidery thread
• Embroidery needle
• Punch needle or knitting needle (to make a hole)
• A length of twine

**1** • Fold a fairly dense batt of white wool in half to get a straight line along the top, then fold the bottom under to form a curve. Felt this shape firmly until it has an even thickness of approximately 4mm (a little less than ¼in). Form the bird's tail and beak as shown in the photograph.

**2** • Fold two other batts of wool into pointed cones, one slightly larger than the other and felt them as you did for the body. Go back over the edges, pinching the wool as shown in Technique 6 to form neat curves. Leave the corollas loose so you can attach the wings to the body.

**3** • Attaching the wings to the body using the corollas is done a little differently from when you are working on a 3D shape. Divide each corolla in half and spread half the wool over the top of the body, and the other half underneath it. Before felting the wings into place, make sure that the centre of each wing is correctly positioned on the body.

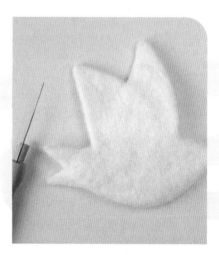

**4** • To form the second point of the dove's tail, felt a small cone of wool separately, then flatten it. Attach it to the rest of the body using the same technique as you did for the wings.

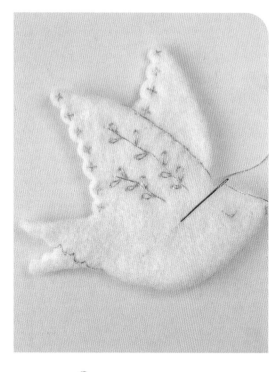

**5** • To scallop the edges of the dove's wings and tail, use Technique 6 once again, poking several times in the same place, every 5mm (¼in) or so. Watch your fingers!

**6** • Next embroider the foliage on the dove's wings and the little crosses along the edges. I used stem stitch, running stitch and daisy stitch.

**7** • All that remains is to gently pierce a hole in the tip of your dove's wing, using a punch needle or knitting needle, and to thread some twine through the hole to create a hanging loop.

# MATRIOCHKAS

These nesting dolls, of Slavic origin, are known throughout the world. They are made of hand-painted linden wood. They are distant cousins of the Japanese Darumas, which were in turn imported by Chinese monks. Symbols of maternity and fertility, these dolls contain as many as seven ever smaller dolls, sometimes more, and can often be real works of art.

## Wool

• White wool
• Handful of dark yellow wool
• Handful of raspberry-coloured wool
• Handful of red wool
• Wisps of coral-coloured, pink and black wool

To give an idea of quantities, the large doll weighs 9g, the medium 5g and the small 3g.

## Equipment

• One medium 40-gauge needle and one fine 42-gauge needle
• Felting pen fitted with three 40-gauge needles

**Difficulty level :**
A project for learning how to reproduce a single 3D design at different scales and manage the different quantities of wool you need.

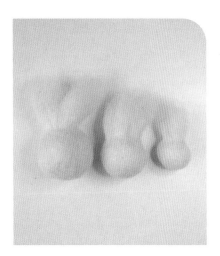

**1** • Using approximately three quarters of your white wool, form three balls with corollas, one large, one medium-sized and one small, following Technique 4.

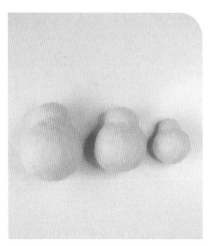

**2** • Wind some strips of white wool around the corollas and fold them as shown in the photo, to form the dolls' heads. Felt the whole thing firmly and deeply; this will make the subsequent process of applying decoration simpler and neater.

**3** • Apply a fine layer of coloured wool to the shoulders of each doll to form the bottom part of their shawls. Try to shape symmetrical curves at the front, slanting downwards a little to form a point at the back. Choose a different colour shawl for each matriochka.

**4** • Apply matching wool to the top of the each doll's head, leaving a round white space for the face, as shown in the photo.

**5** • Roll two little balls of pink wool and attach to form the cheeks, up against the shawl.

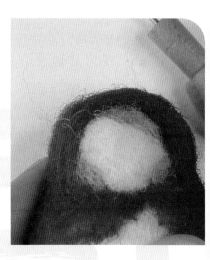

**6** • For the hair, apply a small batt of coral-coloured wool at the top of the face, at an angle.

**7** • Roll two tiny black balls then attach them to form the eyes. Form the mouth in the same way with two small red balls touching each other. If necessary, refer back to Technique 7 for advice about attaching small decorative elements.

**8** • Using two colours that are different from the shawl colour, decorate the stomach of each of your dolls. I have chosen to use two little hearts set symmetrically either side of a larger heart. In the photo, you can see the work in progress: first I fixed one side of the heart, then the other, pulling on the wool to make two nice curves at the top of my hearts.

### Pattern for design detail

**9** • Complete the decoration of your dolls by positioning some large spots of white wool randomly over their shawls.

### Note

It is a good exercise to try to reproduce a single design at different scales. Play around with alternating the colours to make a consistent, matching series of matriochkas that go together, even if they are all a little different.

# THE WISE MONKEYS

These little monkeys, born of Confucian Chinese wisdom, are so famous they have even become emojis! But do you know their names? Let me introduce Kikazaru (the deaf), Iwazaru (the mute) and Mizaru (the blind). Far from telling us to ignore bad things, these three monkeys are advocating that we should not allow negative things to affect us, and should not use our words or deeds to allow them to spread.

**Difficulty level :** ●●
A project where you will learn to create a matching set and get practice in making repeated identical shapes and managing the amounts of wool you use.

## Wool

• 2g of brown wool
• 2g of caramel-coloured wool
• 2g of beige wool
• Batt of cream wool
• Pinch of black wool
• Wisp of coral-coloured wool

## Equipment

• One medium 40-gauge needle and one fine 42-gauge needle
• Felting pen fitted with three 40-gauge needles
• Foam mat

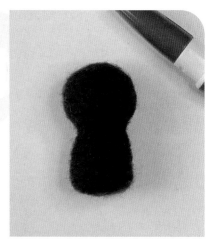

**1 •** Use Technique 4 to form each monkey's head in the shape of a slightly flattened ball, with a healthy corolla underneath.

**2 •** Roll wool the same colour as the head around the corolla and felt hard to shape your monkey's body. It should be the same height as the head, but narrower and slightly conical.

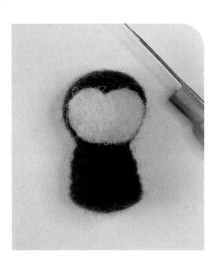

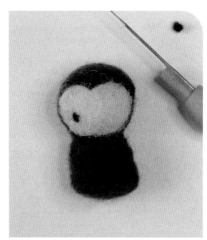

**3 •** Felt a batt of cream-coloured wool to the face, forming a kind of large heart shape that is rounded at the base. Use a single needle to ensure a neat outline.

**4 •** For the eyes, roll some small balls of black wool between your fingers, then attach on either side of the face, referring to Technique 7.

**5 •** Again referring to Technique 7, use the coral-coloured wool for the nose.

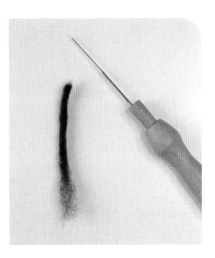

**6 •** Using Technique 2, make two rounded ears separately by folding a small batt of wool in half on a foam mat, then felting them, fanning out the corolla that you will have taken care to leave free at the base to attach to either side of the head.

**7 •** Felt two cylindrical legs, rolling up the wool as shown in the photo. Attach the two little crossed legs at the bottom of the body by poking repeatedly into the edges of the cylinders so they fuse as much as possible with the wool of the body.

**8 •** Twist a narrow strip of wool to form the tail and fix the twist in place by felting the tail on a foam mat.

**10 •** Finish by making the arms and attaching them in the position of your choice, depending on whether you are making the deaf, blind or mute monkey.

**9 •** Coil one end of the tail and poke to hold the loop in place, then attach the tail to the body, having fanned out the corolla as you did for the ears in step 6.

# UKRAINIAN EGG

*The fragility of decorated Ukrainian eggs, known as* pysanky, *as well as the virtuosity of the specialist artists who make them, have always fascinated me. I have been lucky enough to learn to make the real things with a technique that uses acid dye and hot wax. This requires a steady hand and a great deal of patience! This carded wool version of the '40 triangles' design (in reality 48!) does not take anywhere near as long.*

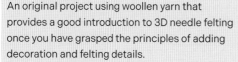

**Difficulty level :** ● ●
An original project using woollen yarn that provides a good introduction to 3D needle felting once you have grasped the principles of adding decoration and felting details.

## Wool

• White woollen yarn
• 20g of light tan-coloured wool
• Small batt of black wool
• Small batt of red wool

The quantity of wool is more important in this project than for others in this book. To start with I would recommend you make a large egg as I have done (approximately the size of a goose's egg) before making smaller versions, about the size of hens' eggs.

## Equipment

• One medium 40-gauge needle and one fine 42-gauge needle
• Felting pen fitted with three 40-gauge needles

**1** • Start by making a light tan-coloured egg and felting it very hard. Make sure that the wool is tightly packed from the start to save you time felting and allow you to form your shape quickly. It is a very similar to making a ball as described in Technique 4, except you do not keep the corolla and you are aiming for an egg shape rather than a sphere.

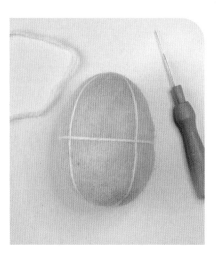

**2** • Attach lengths of white woollen yarn to your egg, using the 42-gauge needle to poke along the ends of the yarn without splitting it too much. Take your time. Divide your egg vertically into four, forming a right-angled cross at the top. Then divide it in half horizontally. At the joins, overlap your yarn for a few millimetres and felt.

**3** • Take the yarn round diagonally from the central crosses, twice, as shown in the photo. Go right round the egg each time.

**4** • Add another couple of rounds of yarn in the same way after rotating your egg a quarter of a turn. You should obtain the same pattern as in the photo.

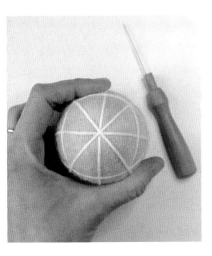

**5** • Look at the cross on the top of your egg. Add another two rounds of yarn to form the diagonals of the cross at the top. Your egg is now divided into 48 regular triangles! Fascinating, isn't it?

**6** • Now felt a fine layer of black wool in every other triangle to give relief to your decoration. Use a 42-gauge needle to make the outlines of each black triangle sharp without encroaching on the white yarn.

**7** • Add a few red triangles as shown in the photo and your egg is complete!

**Note**

Try searching *pysanky* on Google to discover the multitude of traditional patterns possible. You will see that they are always symmetrical and break down into simple components. All of them can be made in carded wool. With a bit of patience, you could make yourself quite a collection!

# REPEÏNIK

Repeïnik *is the Slavic name for the plant that we call the giant burdock. Its seeds are in the form of tiny hooks. This enables them to disperse by clinging to our shoes and socks, as well as animal fur, which is how they reached the pages of this book. According to Slavic beliefs, wearing this amulet allows you to 'hook' (attract) success and happiness. I hope this little character makes you laugh, which is certainly the first step on the road to happiness!*

Creation by @julieadore
www.julieadore.blogspot.com

## Wool

• 5g of green wool
• Pinch of black wool
• Pinch of mauve wool

## Equipment

• One medium 40-gauge needle and one fine 42-gauge needle
• Felting pen fitted with three 40-gauge needles
• Embroidery needle
• Embroidery thread in various shades of mauve
• Pair of very sharp sewing scissors

**Difficulty level :** ⬤
A project that combines felting and embroidery; great for starting work on figurines.

**1 •** Form a large ball with the green wool and wrap one end in a very tightly rolled batt of the same coloured wool. Felt all the way round. You should obtain the result shown in the photo.

**2 •** Snip off the opposite end to the bulb cleanly. In principle, I never advise you to cut a wool shape. However, in this specific case, the cut end will be hidden by the flower's petals eventually and we simply need it to be very flat. Felt the cut surface to work in the fibres as much as possible, using the felting pen.

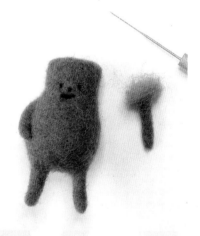

**3 •** Following Technique 7, apply the eyes, nose and smile as shown in the photo. Use tiny quantities of black wool and take your time – a nice expression is often a matter of a single millimetre!

**4 •** Felt some tightly rolled cones of green wool to make the arms and legs, leaving the corolla loose at one end. Attach each limb as shown in the photo, fanning out the corolla against the body of your *repeïnik*.

**5** • For your flower's petals, use as many strands of thread as you can fit through the eye of your embroidery needle. Insert and bring out your needle to make a loop, then pass the two ends of the thread through this loop and pull tight. When the whole head is densely covered to give a lovely, tousled effect, you can move on to the styling! Give your *repeinik* a nice haircut.

**6** • For the final touch, felt a small heart in mauve wool to the chest of your good-luck charm.

# SWEDISH HORSE

I have always adored these little horses from Dalarna, a place you will know if you have had the good fortune to travel in Sweden. They are said to have been carved by country folk as they sat by the fire during the long winter months. Nowadays, they are still hand made by craftsmen in the small village of Nusnäs. For me, the Dala horses represent part of Christmas folklore, and I am particularly fond of them, especially as they give me the opportunity to offer you the most advanced project in this book.

**Difficulty level :** ●●●
The purpose of this project is to demonstrate how you can make animals without a metal frame, as long as you felt firmly.

## Wool

• 18g of red wool
• Small handful of turquoise wool
• Pinch of white wool
• Pinch of yellow wool

## Equipment

• One medium 40-gauge needle and one fine 42-gauge needle
• Felting pen fitted with three 40-gauge needles
• Pair of very sharp sewing scissors
• Foam mat

**1 •** Roll up around a third of the red wool tightly and felt it deeply without touching the ends. You should obtain a sausage that is flattened on the front and back. These are the beginnings of the horse's legs.

**2 •** Felt hard along the median line to create a groove as shown in the photo.

**3 •** Next comes the most impressive part: cut cleanly through the middle of the shape, to give you the horse's two front and two back legs. Using the felting pen, felt the (cut) base of each pair of legs hard to ensure the ends are neat and stable, working in the cleanly cut fibres, which are never very attractive.

**4 •** To form the horse's torso, make a kind of potato shape, flattened at one end, by felting another third of the red wool, as shown in the photo. Keep moving around the shape to ensure a nicely rounded belly.

**5 •** Attach the front and hind legs to the horse's body, fanning out the corollas and felting them firmly against the body. You can unscrew the top section of the pen as shown in the photo, so your needles sink more deeply into the wool if this helps. Make sure the legs are parallel so the horse can stand up by itself.

**6 •** Take a third of the remaining red wool, roll it up and felt it into a cone with a rounded tip to form the horse's muzzle.

**7 •** Set aside a large pinch of the remaining red wool. Arrange the horse's body and head as shown in the photo, then wrap the batt of the remaining red wool around them to join the body and head and create the neck.

**8 •** Use a small bit of the remaining red wool to make a small cone for the horse's ears; attach slightly forward at the top of the head.

**Tip**

Felt the neckline, visualising the rounded form that you are seeking. In my opinion the charm of these little Dala horses lies in the curve of their necks.

**9 •** Use your last little pinch of red wool to add some volume under your horse's belly, as shown in the photo.

**10 •** You have completed the basic shape. Now comes the fun bit: the decoration. I have chosen to give my horse a saddle in the shape of a turquoise flower with five petals. I used very fine batts of wool, which I radiated out from a central point (a foam mat is useful here), and then felted it onto the horse's back using Technique 2.

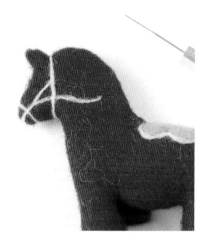

**11** • Roll some little sausages of yellow wool between your fingers to decorate around the saddle and mark the bridle as shown in the photo. Preferably use your 42-gauge needle as it will make your work more accurate.

## 360° views

**12** • Finish decorating your horse however you want, first using small balls of white wool, then turquoise, along the neck and on the saddle and bridle. You have completed your first horse! You can now try some variations in decoration and colour... I bet you can't wait to see your herd multiply!

# MEXICAN CALAVERA

*I was keen for this book to include a calavera, one of the skulls that are found in every possible guise across the whole country of Mexico, on the Day of the Dead. This project is not an easy one, but don't panic; think of it as a training exercise. And don't hesitate to resort to embroidery if you feel you have reached your limits.*

**Creation by @zakadit**
www.zakadit.com

**Difficulty level :** ● ● ●
A project teaching you how to interpret a carded-wool design and make progress in applying fine decoration to flat felting.

## Wool

• 3g of white wool
• Handful of black wool
• Small quantities of navy blue, red, pink, yellow, green and orange wool

## Equipment

• One medium 40-gauge needle and one fine 42-gauge needle
• Felting pen fitted with three 40-gauge needles
• Steam iron
• Brooch back

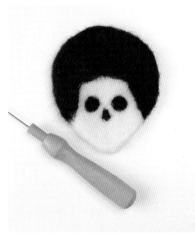

**1 •** Take a batt of white wool and fold the edges under until you have a flat egg shape. Felt the two sides flat, using Technique 2 to obtain a smooth finish. Felt the edges using Technique 6.

**2 •** Place fine but dense batts of black wool as hair, eye sockets and nose hole, as shown in the photo. Referring to Technique 7, felt the edges delicately to ensure the black wool stays separate from the white wool.

**3 •** From this point on, I would recommend working the details one colour at a time. Start by attaching two yellow semi-circles as earrings under the face at either side. Roll a small strip of yellow wool between your fingers and felt it into place all around the eye sockets.

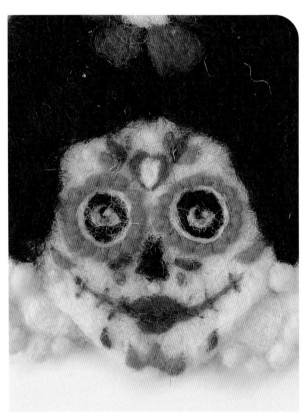

**4 •** Progressively add all the details, taking inspiration from Zak's design as illustrated in the pattern for design detail. This consists of felting a combination of small balls, and fine strands of wool to the face. Follow Technique 7 carefully, making sure the ends of your lines of wool are pulled tight, using the point of your fine 42-gauge needle, before attaching them by gently felting the surface of each detail. The eyes are made up of a white almond shape, followed by a green circle for the iris. The black pupil and white reflection are added over the top in the form of tiny balls of wool.

**5** • Finish by decorating the hair. Then highlight the details by adding narrow borders of navy blue wool along the motifs, in the petals of the flowers, etc. Before sewing the finished piece onto the blank brooch of your choice, you could iron it with a very small amount of steam to firmly fix all the details onto the background wool.

## Pattern for design detail

# EGYPTIAN AMULET

The hippopotamus is a symbol of rebirth because it emerges from water, and is a protective goddess of women in labour in its female version. This animal was omnipresent in the mythology and hieroglyphics of ancient Egypt, even though nowadays you are no longer at risk of encountering one on the banks of the Nile. It was placed with the mummies to accompany them in the afterlife, or worn as an amulet. As someone with a passion for art history, I could not leave Egypt and its magical amulets out of this book!

**Difficulty level :** ●●
The challenge with this project is achieving attractive curves on each part as you add it.

## Wool

• 15g of turquoise wool
• Small handful of black wool
• Small amount of white wool (if you don't have any, some tiny pieces of light-coloured woollen yarn will do the trick)

## Equipment

• One medium 40-gauge needle and one fine 42-gauge needle
• Felting pen fitted with three 40-gauge needles
• Two nuts or bolts (used for internal weights in the animal's body)
• 1 foam mat

**1** • Take three fifths of the turquoise wool and roll it up tightly with the two nuts or bolts inside. Felt into a slightly flattened, firm but springy ball – this will be the hippo's stomach. The bolts will serve as a counterbalance to the head. Take your time and make sure you don't break your needles by stabbing them against the metal.

**2** • Divide the rest of the turquoise wool in half and set aside one portion, using the remaining half to felt four short, cylindrical legs referring to the technique given for Ganesh, steps 4 and 5. Attach the legs in the middle of your hippo's stomach, as close together as to be almost touching. Make sure that they are all the same length.

**3** • Felt the hippo's head from the remaining turquoise wool, keeping just a little bit of the wool separate to make the ears, the snout, the neck wrinkles and the tail later. You should end up with a shape similar to the one shown in the photo; make sure the corolla is located at the top and towards the back of the head. It should be fairly dense in order to make it easy to attach to the body.

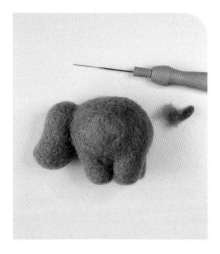

**4** • Felt a jaunty little tail and fix it in the middle of the hippo's hindquarters. In order for the wool to form the curve you want, you need to felt heavily on the concave side: the denser the wool, the more it pulls and forms the curve.

**5 •** Felt two long, small ears separately, making a fold down the middle of each. Attach them well apart, on top of the head.

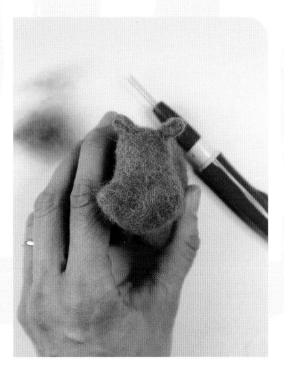

**6 •** Give a little volume to the hippo's snout, by adding wool to the head around the nostrils, which you felt in the form of two small pyramid shapes.

**7 •** Fold, two small, slightly elongated batts of wool in half widthways, and felt in steps under the neck, to resemble the wrinkly folds of the hippo's skin.

**8 •** Now form the eyes by rolling two tiny balls of black wool between your fingers, before putting them into place and attaching them well apart halfway up the head. For the nostrils, roll two very fine, slightly curved sausages of black wool and attach them on each side of the snout.

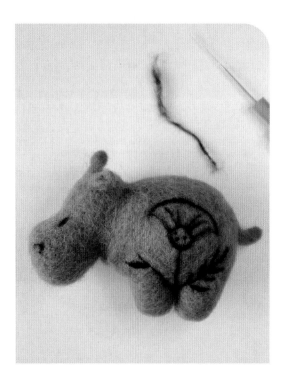

## Pattern for design detail

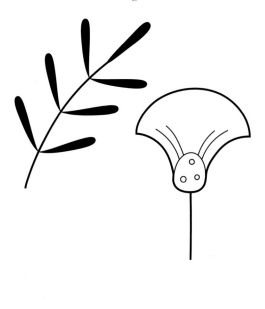

**9 •** You can now decorate your hippo's body as you like. I have opted for stylised palm trees and papyrus flowers. To succeed at this stage, it is important for the hippo's body to have been well felted at step 1 to ensure it is nice and dense, otherwise the decorative details may sink into the man body. Use Technique 7 to fix them into place.

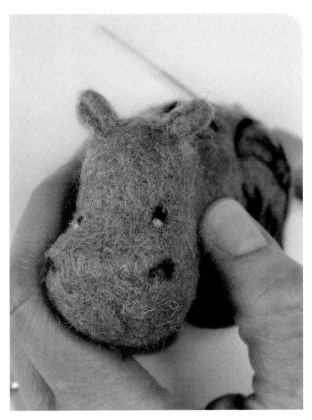

**10** • Finish by adding two tiny spots of white to give your hippo a glint in its eyes. Alternatively, you could buy and attach plastic or glass eyes; personally I prefer what I make to be 100% wool, but very tiny decorative details require a bit of practise before they can be attached without sinking. Once again, patience is key.

## 360° views

# CACTUS PINCUSHION

*I wanted to pay homage in this book to all the dressmakers who have inspired my love of needlecraft. The idea of a pincushion seemed like a natural choice. So here is a soft, colourful little talisman to keep you company while you sew.*

Creation by @happy_as_a_bee_
www.happy-as-a-bee.com

**Difficulty level :** ●●
A project teaching you how to recycle your wool and how to make straight indented lines.

## Wool

• Some leftover balls of wool and/or the remnants of carded wool for recycling
• 2g of green wool (I used combed wool but you can also use carded wool)
• 8g approximately of orange wool
• Small handful of deep pink wool
• Scraps of wool in different shades of pink and white

## Equipment

• One medium 40-gauge needle
• Felting pen fitted with three 40-gauge needles
• Sewing needle and thread

**1 •** Wrap some tiny balls of leftover wool in tails of woollen yarn to create three elongated balls, which will act as the base for each branch of your cactus. Vary the size of each branch so you have three different sizes. To cover these balls of recycled wool, I have used combed wool roving arranged in a cross shape, which I have folded over the balls to hide them.

**Tip**

As soon as you start working with carded wool, you will often have mixed bits of leftover roving to recycle. Never throw anything away!

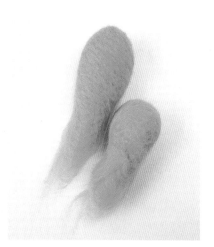

**2 •** Felt the full length of the surface area with the felting pen, adding wool if necessary to completely hide the recycled wool beneath. The finish is a bit more fibrous and is slightly longer than if you used carded wool, because here the fibres are parallel and so less mixed at the start than in a carded batt. Leave long corollas at the base of each branch; they will be used to attach the pot.

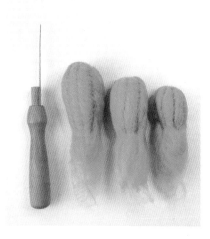

**3 •** To create the relief on the surface of the cactus, work a single 40-gauge needle down in vertical lines, poking at close intervals. Spend some time going along each groove several times. You will gradually see the texture emerge. The result is very satisfying.

**4** • Keeping the corollas of the three branches of your cactus squeezed tightly together, wrap them in the batt of orange wool to create the pot. Felt using Tip 6 (see My Top 10 Tips) to obtain the vertical edges and a perpendicular, horizontal base. Add wool until your pot is the desired size. The secret is to ensure the wool is tight from the start and to felt each layer firmly.

**5** • To decorate your pot, place fine layers of pink wool vertically on the pot and then felt them delicately to the surface, using your single needle. Refer to Technique 7.

**6** • Separately, felt a small circle of wool in various shades of pink and white, and scallop the edges with the single needle (see step 5 of the Dove of Peace). Fix this flower firmly on top of one of the branches of your cactus. I would recommend stitching it on as well to ensure it is firmly attached.

## 360° views

# KAWAII PANDA

An Asian symbol of the balance of strength and wisdom, its colours reminiscent of yin and yang, this book would not be complete without a panda – never mind their cute little faces! I asked my community to suggest some designs for their perfect panda… They were all adorable but I chose this design because I find it interesting to try to reproduce a particular expression and posture – in this case, a yawning panda!

Creation by @lysca_illustration

**Difficulty level :** ●●●
If you like creating your own models based on characters from cartoons or an illustrated book, this project should serve as inspiration.

## Wool

• 8g of white wool
• 3g of dark grey wool
• Pinch of black wool
• Pinch of red wool

## Equipment

• One medium 40-gauge needle and one fine 42-gauge needle
• Felting pen fitted with three 40-gauge needles

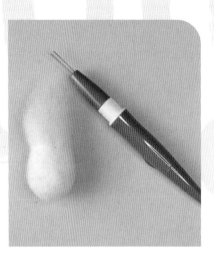

**1 •** Using approximately two thirds of the white wool, make an oblong shape for the body, referring to Technique 4. Fold the corolla against the shape itself, to obtain a kind of potato shape.

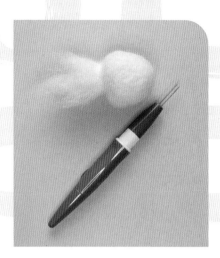

**2 •** Using the same technique, make the head separately. Try and make it so the bottom of the ball is a little larger than the top so you can make the cheeks. If necessary, add wool a little bit at a time over this area.

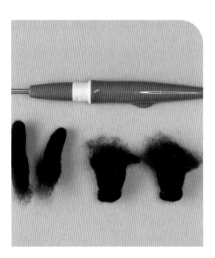

**3 •** To make the arms and legs, roll small quantities of dark grey wool into separate, tight cones, then felt. The legs should be wider and shorter than the arms. Felt the underside of the paws perpendicularly to the legs, turning the shape as you poke round the ankles to define them clearly, as shown in the photo, following Tip 5 in My Top 10 Tips.

**4 •** Fanning out the corolla of the head over the top of the body, attach the two together. I would recommend that you use this method, rather than forming it around the corolla of the head as you would normally, in order to balance the amounts more effectively, because the aim of this project is to interpret a specific design and not to make a generic panda.

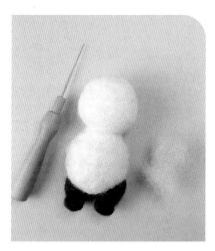

**5** • Attach the back legs to the body. Make sure that your panda can stand upright by itself. Add white wool around the stomach and at the top of the legs, to hide the join and recreate the rounded tummy. Joining two very contrasting colours is not easy, because you need to avoid bringing up the dark colour through the light one. Make sure the grey wool corollas are as deep inside the white wool as possible to prevent the fibres from being seen on the surface; felt deeply with a single needle.

**6** • Before attaching the arms, give them the required curve, poking repeatedly around the wrists and elbows. The more you poke down one side of an arm, the more it will curve inwards because the wool will compress in the area where you are working and pull on the shape as a whole. You will find that little by little you will learn instinctively where to work in order to achieve the curves you want.

**7** • Remember that your figurine is 3D so do not forget to work, or rather to imagine, the back. In the illustration for this design, I could only see the panda's front, but I added some volume around the thighs and, of course, the strip of dark grey on the upper back that is common to all pandas.

**8** • To make the face, add small amounts of white wool around the muzzle and lower lip. Add two dark grey, curved comma shapes on either side of the nose. Felt two little teardrop-shaped ears separately and attach them behind the head, as shown in the photo.

**9** • Felt a little bit of black inside the mouth and two eyes in the form of sideways commas. Finally, add a ball of black wool to the tip of the nose, attaching it as described in Tip 3 (see My Top 10 Tips) and felt a little red tongue into the open mouth.

## 360° views

# SUMMARY TABLE

*For each project, this table gives the suppliers and references for the wool used, the dimensions of the felted piece, the stages of learning and the level of difficulty.*

| Project | Supplier | Reference | Dimensions | Learning | Level |
|---|---|---|---|---|---|
| **Sakura**<br>Page 28 | Ô Merveille ! | White | 6 x 5cm<br>(2⅜ x 2in) | A beginner's project that combines embroidery, beads and felted wool, and provides an introduction to mixing colours. | * |
| | Ô Merveille ! | Petal | | | |
| | DMC Diamant thread | D301 | | | |
| | DMC Diamant thread | D225 | | | |
| **Ganesh**<br>Page 32 | Ô Merveille ! | Sand | 8 x 6.5 x 4cm<br>(3⅛ x 2½ x 2in) | A project to practise making little *kawaii* animals. | ** |
| | Ô Merveille ! | Curry | | | |
| | Ô Merveille ! | Corn | | | |
| | DHG Shop | Carded Maori wool – Yolk | | | |
| | DHG Shop | Carded Maori wool – Lipstick | | | |
| | Ô Merveille ! | Pumpkin | | | |
| | Ô Merveille ! | Thunderstorm | | | |
| **Four-leaf clover**<br>Page 40 | Ô Merveille ! | Leaf green | 3.5 x 3.5cm<br>(1⅜ x 1⅜in) | A beginner's project to help you get to grips with flat felting using a mould. This technique allows you to achieve a complex shape quite easily. | * |
| | Ô Merveille ! | Moss green | | | |
| **Hand of Fatima**<br>Page 44 | Ô Merveille ! | Black | 8 x 7.5cm<br>(3⅛ x 3in) | A beginner's project to try out flat felting without a mould, start adding details and learn to work neatly in very contrasting wools. | * |
| | Ô Merveille ! | White | | | |
| **Evil eye**<br>Page 48 | Ô Merveille ! | Ultramarine blue | 7 x 6cm<br>(2¾ x 2⅜in) | An easy project for a stress-free introduction to needle felting. | * |
| | Ô Merveille ! | Duck blue | | | |
| | Ô Merveille ! | White | | | |
| | Ô Merveille ! | Black | | | |
| **Maneki-neko**<br>Page 52 | Ô Merveille ! | Black | 8 x 5 x 3.5cm<br>(3⅛ x 2 x 1⅜in) | Very detailed step-by-step instructions make this the ideal project for creating your first *amigurumi* in carded wool. | ** |
| | Ô Merveille ! | White | | | |
| | Ô Merveille ! | Curry | | | |
| | Ô Merveille ! | Red | | | |
| | Ô Merveille ! | Coral | | | |
| | Ô Merveille ! | Caramel | | | |

| Project | Brand | Colour | Dimensions | Description | Difficulty |
|---|---|---|---|---|---|
| **Sacred Heart** Page 60 | Meaningful Crafts | Bheda wool – Fresh mint | 9 x 6cm (3½ x 2⅜in) | A project to help you progress your flat felting, and which confirms that you really can decorate anything with carded wool! | ** |
| | Ô Merveille ! | Red | | | |
| | Ô Merveille ! | Raspberry | | | |
| | Ô Merveille ! | Duck blue | | | |
| | Ô Merveille ! | Curry | | | |
| **Ladybird** Page 64 | Ô Merveille ! | Red | 4.5 x 3.5cm (1¾ x 1⅜in) | A very simple project teaching you how to felt over a metal frame. | * |
| | Ô Merveille ! | Black | | | |
| **Dolphin** Page 68 | Meaningful Crafts | Bheda – Pastel blue | 8.5 x 6.5 x 5.5cm (3¼ x 2½ x 2¼in) | A project to help you learn how to model simple shapes and connect them together. | * |
| | Ô Merveille ! | Black | | | |
| | Ô Merveille ! | White | | | |
| | Ô Merveille ! | Petal | | | |
| **Daruma** Page 72 | Ô Merveille ! | Red | 6 x 5.5 x 4.5cm (2⅜ x 2¼ x 1¾in) | An interesting project for starting out in 3D felting. | * |
| | Ô Merveille ! | Black | | | |
| | Ô Merveille ! | Biscuit | | | |
| | Meaningful Crafts | Carded fleece – Mountain sheep wool white | | | |
| **Dove of peace** Page 76 | Meaningful Crafts | Carded fleece – Mountain sheep wool white | 11 x 12cm (4¼ x 4¾in) | The challenge of this project lies in taking time to master the complex flat-felted shapes and managing the proportions so the angles formed at the points of attachment remain faithful to the design. | ** |
| | DMC Diamant thread | D3852 | | | |
| **Matriochkas** Page 80 | Ô Merveille ! | White | Height : 6.5cm (2½in) / 5cm (2in) / 3.5cm (1⅜in) | A project for learning how to reproduce a single 3D design at different scales and manage the different quantities of wool you need. | * |
| | Pain d'Epices | Fuchsia | | | |
| | Ô Merveille ! | Curry | | | |
| | Ô Merveille ! | Red | | | |
| | Ô Merveille ! | Malabar | | | |
| | Ô Merveille ! | Coral | | | |
| | Ô Merveille ! | Black | | | |
| **The wise monkeys** Page 84 | Ô Merveille ! | Chestnut | 3.5 x 3.5 x 1.5cm (1⅜ x 1⅜ x ⅝in) | A project where you will learn to create a matching set and get practice in making repeated identical shapes and managing the amounts of wool you use. | ** |
| | Ô Merveille ! | Red | | | |
| | Créalia | Taupe | | | |
| | Ô Merveille ! | Flesh | | | |
| | Ô Merveille ! | Coral | | | |
| | Ô Merveille ! | Black | | | |
| **Ukrainian egg** Page 88 | Ô Merveille ! | Flesh | 9 x 6 x 6cm (3½ x 2⅜ x 2⅜in) | An original project using woollen yarn that provides a good introduction to 3D needle felting once you have grasped the principles of adding decoration and felting details. | ** |
| | Ô Merveille ! | Black | | | |
| | Ô Merveille ! | Red | | | |

| | | | | | |
|---|---|---|---|---|---|
| **Repeïnik**<br>Page 92 | Ô Merveille ! | Fir green | 10 x 4 x 3cm<br>(4 x 1½ x 1⅛in) | A project that combines felting and embroidery; great for starting work on figurines. | * |
| | Créalia | Deep purple | | | |
| | Ô Merveille ! | Black | | | |
| **Swedish horse**<br>Page 96 | Ô Merveille ! | Red | 12 x 13 x 3.5cm<br>(4¾ x 5 x 1⅜in) | The purpose of this project is to demonstrate how you can make animals without a metal frame, as long as you felt firmly. | *** |
| | DHG Shop | Sun | | | |
| | Meaningful Crafts | European merino lontwol – Turquoise | | | |
| **Mexican calavera**<br>Page 102 | Meaningful Crafts | Carded fleece – Mountain sheep wool white | 8.5 x 7cm<br>(3¼ x 2¾in) | A project teaching you how to interpret a carded-wool design and make progress in applying fine decoration to flat felting. | *** |
| | Ô Merveille ! | Black | | | |
| | Ô Merveille ! | Red | | | |
| | Pain d'Epices | Orange | | | |
| | Ô Merveille ! | Navy | | | |
| | DHG Shop | Carded Maori wool – Sun | | | |
| | DHG Shop | Carded Maori wool – Lipstick | | | |
| | Pain d'Epices | Vert vif | | | |
| **Egyptian amulet**<br>Page 106 | Ô Merveille ! | Duck blue | 10 x 5 x 6cm<br>(4 x 2 x 2⅜in) | The challenge with this project is achieving attractive curves on each part as you add it. | ** |
| | Ô Merveille ! | Black | | | |
| | Ô Merveille ! | White | | | |
| **Cactus pincushion**<br>Page 112 | Meaningful Crafts | European merino wool – Turquoise | 9.5 x 4 x 4cm<br>(3¾ x 1½ x 1½in) | A project teaching you how to recycle your wool and how to make straight indented lines. | ** |
| | Ô Merveille ! | Pumpkin | | | |
| | Ô Merveille ! | Raspberry | | | |
| | Ô Merveille ! | White | | | |
| | Pain d'Epices | Fuchsia | | | |
| **Kawaii panda**<br>Page 116 | Ô Merveille ! | White | 10 x 5 x 4.5cm<br>(4 x 2 x 1¾in) | If you like creating your own models based on characters from cartoons or an illustrated book, this project should serve as inspiration. | *** |
| | Ô Merveille ! | Steel grey | | | |
| | Ô Merveille ! | Black | | | |
| | Ô Merveille ! | Red | | | |

# USEFUL ADDRESSES AND RESOURCES

## NEEDLE FELTING SUPPLIERS

### UK and Europe

Ö Merveille: https://www.omerveille.com/fr/ (whom we thank for supplying much of the wool used in this book)
DHG shop: https://www.dhgshop.it/index_eng.php
Meaningful Crafts: https://meaningfulcrafts.com/
Pain d'Épices: https://www.paindepices.fr/store/Laine/Kits-Ours-Pain-d-Epices
The Felt Box: https://thefeltbox.uk/
The Makerss: https://www.themakerss.co.uk/

### North America

Living Felt: https://feltingsupplies.livingfelt.com/
The Woolery: https://woolery.com/
Fibrecraft: https://fibrecraft.ca/

### Australia

The Thread Collective: https://threadcollective.com.au/collections/felting-tools
The Wool Room: https://www.thewoolroom.com.au/c/spinning-weaving-felting/

## OTHER SUPPLIERS

Clover for plastic 3-needle felting pens: https://www.clover-mfg.com/
DMC for embroidery threads: https://www.dmc.com

## OTHER RESOURCES

The Field Guide to Fleece: 100 Sheep Breeds & How to Use Their Fibers, Deborah Robson and Carol Ekarius (Storey Publishing, 2013)
Wild Colour: How to Make and Use Natural Dyes, Jenny Dean (Mitchell Beazeley, 2018)
The Felt Museum, Mouzon: https://www.mouzon.fr/culture-et-patrimoine/musee-du-feutre/

# INTRODUCTION TO THE GUEST CREATORS

**I couldn't finish this book without telling you a little about each of the creations that my fellow crafters have done the honour of designing for my needles.**

### Julie Adore
@julieadore – www.julieadore.blogspot.com

*I asked my friend Julie to tell me what her lucky charm would be. She produced a design based on one of the ancient talismans of Slavic popular culture, the repeïnik. It is a giant burdock plant. Its seeds hook themselves to our shoes or passing animals. Wearing this amulet attracts success and happiness.*

### Zakadit
@zakadit – www.zakadit.com

*I wanted a Mexican calavera in this book and it seemed obvious to me, following the first Frida Kahlo tutorial that we did together, to ask Zak to design it. But when I received his gorgeous design, I realised that it wasn't going to be all that easy to do! Cheeky Zak had thrown down an attractive gauntlet, but I seized it!*

### Ombeline Brun
@ombeline_brun – www.ombelinebrun.com

*My friend Ombeline Brun, whose woodworking I greatly admire, was kind enough to let me interpret her iconic dove in wool. We had already collaborated with her babies. I was really touched to have been able to mix my wool with her delicate designs once again. And for some time now, she has been adding woollen touches to what she makes... that makes me so proud!*

### Lysca Illustration
@lysca_illustration

*Léa is an illustrator and paper artist. I discovered her work during a miniature challenge that I launched online in early 2023. Blown away by the expressive nature of her creations, it was no surprise at how delighted I was when I saw the panda she had designed in response to my call.*

### Ginacie
@ginacie – www.ginacie.blogspot.com

*Melanie has a universe of folklore and enchantment that is all her own. I love her style as much as her pertinent words on our lives as women and mothers. When I wanted a Sacred Heart design, there was no-one better placed than her to do the job!*

### Happy as a bee
@happy_as_a_bee – www.happy-as-a-bee.com

*Valentine is an unparalleled dressmaker. Needlework in all its forms holds no secrets for her. I knew that she had already felted on jumpers and we had done a tutorial together on making a super-cute teddy bear. Her heart-warming watercolours are always cheerful, I knew that a pincushion might inspire her.*

### So Croch'
@socroch – www.socroch.fr

*I imagine that many readers of this book are also big fans of crochet amigurumi. When I think of a 'little kawaii animal', my mind immediately jumps to my friend Marie. She was kind enough to accept the challenge and create this duo of crocheted/carded wool dolphins. You can find the tutorial for the crochet version on her site.*

# ACKNOWLEDGEMENTS

*Thanks to the Slavic grandmothers I met on my travels who were needle felting little toys on the metro – and who piqued my curiosity. Thank you, Julie, for how beautiful you make my creations look through your lens. Thank you, Agnès, for your advice and constant encouragement and your beautiful material. Thank you to Pascale, up there, for believing in me and opening the doors of Marabout to me. Thank you to Emmanuelle for her trust. Thank you to my editors, Aude and Emmanuelle, I am so proud to have had the chance to work under your kindly, expert gaze. Thanks to you, Camille, for your off-the-record opinions, which are always so accurate and valuable. Thank you to the breeders for this wonderfully exciting and infinitely soft material that you produce for us. And thank you to all of you, who, in my workshops, in person, online or on Instagram, have joined me in a passion for the infinite possibilities of carded wool; this book is dedicated to you so you can create objects that will offer a little piece of yourself to those you love.*

David and Charles is an imprint of David and Charles, Ltd, Suite A, Tourism House, Pynes Hill, Exeter, EX2 5WS

© Hachette Livre (Marabout) 2023

First published in the UK and USA in 2024

Héléna Zaïchik has asserted her right to be identified as author of this work in accordance with the Copyright, Designs and Patents Act, 1988.

A catalogue record for this book is available from the British Library.

ISBN-13: 9781446314623 paperback
ISBN-13: 9781446314630 EPUB

This book has been printed on paper from approved suppliers and made from pulp from sustainable sources.

Printed in China through Asia Pacific Offset for:
David and Charles, Ltd
Suite A, Tourism House, Pynes Hill, Exeter, EX2 5WS

10 9 8 7 6 5 4 3 2 1

Illustrations on pages 16-17, 22-23: Marion Taslé
Photographs: Julie Robert, other than the step-by-step photos (Héléna Zaïchik) and page 4: Fanny Faria for Artesane; page 101: Marie-Gabrielle Berland; page 9 (from top to bottom): Michelle Provençal, Winnie Chui, Nastasya Shulyak, Marta Cortada; page 13 © Shutterstock
Page-setting: Studio Smarthe
Editorial support: Emmanuelle de Villedary

All the models have been created by Héléna Zaïchik, other than those on pages: 60 (© Ginacie), 68 (© Socroch); 76 (© Ombeline Brun); 92 (© Julie Adore); 102 (© Zakadit); 112 (© Happy as a bee) and 116 (© Lysca Illustration)

Full-size printable versions of the templates are available to download free from www.bookmarkedhub.com. Search for this book by the title or ISBN: the files can be found under 'Book Extras'. Membership of the Bookmarked online community is free.

David and Charles publishes high-quality books on a wide range of subjects. For more information visit www.davidandcharles.com.

Share your makes with us on social media using #dandcbooks and follow us on Facebook and Instagram by searching for @dandcbooks.

Layout of the digital edition of this book may vary depending on reader hardware and display settings.